BROOKHAVEN
WE
2960
MA
S0-ADZ-373

A Promise is to Keep

MARY TEEGARDIN

A PROMISE IS TO KEEP

© 1999 Overseas Missionary Fellowship (*formerly China Inland Mission*)
Published by OMF International (U.S.)
10 West Dry Creek Circle, Littleton, CO 80120-4413.

All rights reserved. Printed in the United States of America. No part of this book may be used or reproduced in any form or by any means, or stored in a database or retrieval system, without prior written permission of the publisher except in the case of brief quotations embodied in critical articles and reviews. Making copies of any part of this book for any purpose other than your own personal use is a violation of United States copyright laws. For information address OMF International, 10 West Dry Creek Circle, Littleton, CO 80120-4413.

Published 2000

OMF Books ISBN 1-929122-03-9
CLC ISBN 0-87508-490-7

OMF Books are distributed by:
OMF, 10 West Dry Creek Circle, Littleton, CO 80120, U.S.A.
OMF, 5759 Coopers Avenue, Mississauga, ON L4Z 1R9, Canada
OMF, Station Approach, Borough Green, Sevenoaks, Kent TN15 8BG, UK
and other OMF offices.

Christian Literature Crusade:
PO Box 1449, Fort Washington, PA 19034, U.S.A.
51 The Dean, Alresford, Hants. SO24 9BJ, UK
PO Box 419M, Manuda, QLD 4879, Australia
10 MacArthur Street, Feilding, New Zealand

This special OMF Books edition is available worldwide through

CHRISTIAN • LITERATURE • CRUSADE

Foreword

"No field or garden yields a harvest without long months of fatiguing and often heart-breaking labor." So writes Mary Tee-gardin as she relates a lesson she needed to learn to sustain her on a remarkable journey of service to God.

I sensed in me a nagging fear as I read *A Promise Is to Keep*—a fear that some will regard it as merely one more missionary tale, good for those who want to satisfy curiousity about mission life or to experience a moment of wonder over how God works.

This is *not* just one more missionary story. It is *not* designed to satisfy the curious or titillate bored Christians. It is the record of God's faithfulness to a woman whose determination to keep her promise was deeper than emotional pain, physical hardship, and torturing questions.

I am a psychologist, a Christian psychologist. I regard it as my main task to help people discover what is deeper, more real, and more important than all their troubles. I do not see it as my central job to solve problems. I long to be guided of God to use people's problems to help them find God, to discover His love, to see their lives as part of a larger story being told by a purposeful and kind Lord.

I know Mary Teegardin personally. When I visited my parents in the same community where Mary resides, it was always a priority of mine and my wife's to spend time with her. Her life is evidence that God does His grandest work in the hearts of those who are abandoned to Him. When I think of Mary, I think of Much-Afraid, the character in *Hinds' Feet on High Places* who moved through her fear to the rich stillness of dwelling in the Shadow of the Almighty. Mary's life, as I have experienced her personally and now have read about her in this book, brings great hope in what God is doing.

I cannot imagine someone reading Mary's book and not being drawn into that larger Story. Don't read *A Promise Is to Keep* without pondering the value of a life lived for God, without reflecting on what life is really about and who God is. Read it with a heart open to God's Spirit—and you will be changed.

Lawrence J. Crabb, Jr., Ph.D.
Littleton, Colorado

Acknowledgments

I am grateful to my sister, Ruth Easterday, and my sister-in-law, Dorothea Teegardin, who carefully saved and filed away my letters from China and Thailand. Without those letters to help me recall detail, I could not have written this story.

Many who read and prayed over what I wrote from various corners of Asia over the years have repeatedly encouraged me to bring those stories out of the musty files and put them into book form. So with care I now lift some episodes from my past to share more widely. As I do so, I wish only to exalt the Lord Jesus Christ, for after all, it was He who gave those experiences to me.

Without the assistance of countless friends, this book would never have been in your hands. I am especially indebted to Orpha Cary, Lillian Thorp, Lillian Myers, and Joy Woodhouse for hours of typing and endless encouragements. I am singularly grateful for valuable suggestions from Johanna Posthuma,

Arthur Wilder, and Donald Muchmore. My heartfelt thanks, in fact, to each one who has helped bring this book to completion, not the least editors Fay Goddard, Miriam Levengood, and Mary Elizabeth Tewksbury.

Mary Teegardin
Keystone Heights, Florida

To
my parents,
who also made
—and kept—
a promise.

CONTENTS

ɛ1ɞ

Prelude to Promise

"**M**ary," Mother called from the kitchen, "go to the chicken coop and get me some eggs. I want to make gingerbread for supper."

Plunking down the giant headphones of my father's crystal-radio set, I tugged on my jacket and ran out into the blustery autumn air.

From wooden nests secured to the walls of the hen house, possessive hens eyed me cautiously. First testing the mood of each hen with a sleeved elbow, I slipped my hand under their feathery breasts. Finally, with my pockets filled with warm eggs, I turned to leave.

At that moment a gust of wind caught the door and blew it shut with a bang. A high, wooden latch jolted into place. I was locked in!

Surveying the situation, I wondered if the chickens' water pail would make me tall enough to reach the latch. Tipping the water onto the floor, I mounted the up-turned bucket. Still too short! From that height, however, I spied rivulets of water flowing toward a tiny hatchway in the wall. An inquisitive hen pecked at the wet litter, then slipped out the little door. "Hey, I can do that," I said to no one in particular.

"Are you coming with the eggs?" Mother called urgently.

Hastily I wriggled my five-year-old body through the small hatch. Standing up, I felt my pockets. Horrified, I found not one whole egg! Crushed shells oozed their contents and mixed with the cold, mucky water already fouling my clothes. Through hot tears I spied an impatient supper-maker rounding the corner of the building.

Mother stopped, gasped, then came to me. Taking my slimy hand in hers without a word of reproach, she led me back to the house for a warm bath. She did not mention the incident at our gingerbread-less supper.

Years later, when a horrified Thai nurse-aide trainee brought me thirty-four broken thermometers that she had boiled to sterilize, I remembered Mother's gentle example.

The country home of my childhood and teen-age years teemed with things to discover, places to explore, and lessons to learn. On hot summer days, for instance, the rhythmical drone of Father's honey bees drew me. In spite of repeated warnings to keep away from the tall hives in the apiary, I would creep to the

Prelude to Promise

base of one of those humming hives and lie quietly with my head only inches from the entrance—listening, watching, smelling. I imagined I could see, as Father had described rows of air-conditioning bees, stationed like soldiers along corridors of honeycomb, fanning their wings to keep the wax walls from melting. Fascinated, I watched worker bees spill out and fly away over my head. Others returning from the fields, laden with honey and pollen, dodged past to settle at the doors of their bustling high-rises. House-keeper bees tumbled from the hives onto the grass with their burdens of waxy debris.

While I lay discovering their secrets, those industrious honey makers never stung me. But later, while at play far from the apiary, I stepped on a bee helplessly caught in the grass. It stung me. As I nursed a painful foot, I felt both betrayed and regretful, knowing that, without a stinger, my assailant would die.

After that my rapport with honey bees began to wane. But a certain fearlessness for flying insects remained. It would help me to cope with the scores of "creepy-crawlies" I later encountered in Asia.

I owe much to my father. He never brushed aside my endless questions—and he told superb stories. Many a summer evening I lay on the cool grass near him listening to endless tales while he smoked. I liked the smell of his cigars, and the smoke kept mosquitoes away.

Some nights Father quoted Shakespeare or long portions from Tennyson, Longfellow, or Browning. Sometimes he spun tales of ancient Roman or Greek mythology. I especially liked stories of pioneer days and American Indians. When northern lights flashed like filmy fairies in the darkening sky, he unlocked their mysteries and explained about the constellations that twinkled through the pine branches above us.

Once when we were talking about the moon and the sun, I asked, "Papa, where does the sun go when it sinks behind those trees in the woods?" His eyes squinted against the cigar smoke as he looked down at me, a smile just discernible. "To China, far away to the west, where west becomes east. It's beginning to be day there now," he added, leaving me to puzzle over that one! Could he have wondered if the young inquirer at his side might one day follow that sun to China?

*L*ong winter evenings provided cozy family times I loved. Father usually read in an arm chair by the parlor door. Mother sat in a straight-backed rocker by the warm stove with a mending basket on her lap. Elder brother Preston crouched over the radio drawing crackling sounds, voices, or music from the mysterious box. Middle siblings Ruth and Orville, busy with homework, sat at the library table near a kerosene lamp. Helen and I, the last two in our family, dressed and undressed our dolls or the kittens from a box behind the stove.

Sometimes growing tired of our play, we asked Mother, "Mama, what can we do now?"

Laying down the heavy sock she darned, Mother would suggest a game. "What about 'hide the thimble'?" she might say, and we would dance impatiently while she searched her basket for a spare thimble.

We loved the game. The familiar old living room held lots of shadowy places to conceal the borrowed thimble. Shrieks of delight shattered the peaceful atmosphere each time one of us found the hidden treasure. But at the stroke of eight from the clock on the high mantel, we knew our game was over. "Bedtime," Mother called.

Reluctantly we dressed in our night clothes and dallied until a curt "Hike!" came from Father.

Pulling warm blankets from the backs of chairs near the stove, we wrapped them snugly around us, said our goodnights and scampered to our cold bedroom as quickly as our blanket-bound legs allowed. As we climbed into bed, our fingers groped for the warm,

newspaper-wrapped bricks Mother had put there earlier. We drew them to our feet and soon fell fast
asleep. Though not kissed or tucked in, we felt secure
and loved in quiet, firm ways. Years later, when I
observed a similar lack of outward affection in oriental
homes, I understoond how loving devotion could exist
there too.

On gusty winter days I preferred to play in the
parlor. It was out of bounds, however, without Mother
there, playing the organ or plying her needle on a

quilt. I never tired of looking at pictures in a red, velvet-covered album or stashed in the lower drawer of Mother's desk. From those pictures I reached back into family history. A time-faded picture of a bearded farmer in homemade, high-top leather boots acquainted me with Grandfather Teegardin, and a scratched tin-type of a young surveyor, Grandfather Morley.

One photo I studied endlessly showed Grandfather and Grandmother Teegardin on their golden wedding anniversary in 1911. They sat at a table reading a Bible. I often wondered what it was in the book that gave them such tranquil expressions, but I never asked. Our family seldom talked about religious matters.

From other photos, Mother explained how Grandpa Metz came to live in her home when her mother—my grandmother—remarried. Mother's own father had died when she was eight. Grandpa Metz was the only grandparent I ever really knew.

Mother also told me how Papa had had to withdraw after his first year at the college where they met because of his own father's illness. He went home to manage the family farm. They didn't marry until Mother had completed her training and taught school for several years.

At the very bottom of the drawer lay a large family photo, taken when I was four. Mother did not like that picture and usually hastened to put it away, saying, "I look sick."

Mother *was* ill. She had begun her long struggle with tuberculosis. I don't know just when my young mind began to comprehend why she regularly put her dishes to boil on the back of the kitchen stove after each meal. Surely her carefulness was part of God's means of protecting my life for His purposes. ■

ဆ2ce

Discovery
in the Woods

*I*n my fourth year at school, consolidation of one-
room schools in the township brought unsettling
changes for me. I lost confidence and became
despondent and defensive. Finding it difficult to make
new friends and unable to share my deepest feelings
with others, I yearned for God but did not know how
to find Him. Though I went regularly to Sunday
school with my brothers and sisters, the stories we
heard seemed unrelated to my longings.

In their early married years my parents had been
active in church. Though they kept Sunday as a day of
rest, by my time they rarely attended Sunday services.
We did not hear the Bible read aloud in our home. We
heard prayers spoken only before meals or when
Grandpa Metz came. Though Mother played the organ well and often lifted her rich alto voice in favorite
hymns, I did not understand the meaning of much she

sang. We learned moral and ethical precepts more by example than by words.

I wanted to do right, but deep in my heart I knew I fell short of the poorly-defined standards. The void in my heart deepened until a mortifying experience pushed me to a great and wonderful discovery.

A new immigrant family had moved into our community. On opening day of school Rosa—a petite, olive-skinned girl with hazel eyes—came to our fifth-grade room. As our teacher introduced her, the girl did a princess-like curtsy that diverted attention from her big, frightened eyes. The teacher cleared his throat. "Now," he said, calling us back from our flights of imagination, "Will all of you please stand and say, 'Welcome to our class, Rosa.'"

When that was done, the teacher motioned us to our seats. Classes began. During the morning I sensed an unusual odor in the room. After recess, when all windows stood open, the odor not only persisted, it grew stronger. Sometime during the morning I wrote a note to a friend a few seats away. In it I confided that the smell surely came from our new classmate. "She must be very dirty," I concluded.

At noon the mystery of the strange odor was solved. Garlic! The new family used it freely.

The school bell had scarcely stopped ringing after lunch break when our teacher ordered me to go to the principal's office. The tone of his voice and the expression on his face told me this was no ordinary request to get something from the office.

Panic made my legs wooden. That panic blossomed to near terror when I saw my note on the principal's desk. Sternly, the principal read the words I had written from that crumpled scrap of paper. When he rebuked me for the hurtful things I had penned, I knew I deserved it.

After telling me to apologize to Rosa, the principal dismissed me. No walk was ever so painful as my return to our classroom. Titters and knowing nudges from classmates shamed me.

Wrestling with my dilemma, I delayed my apology until after class. I flung a "I'm sorry," toward Rosa, then hastily climbed onto the waiting school bus. Glancing toward my older sister, I knew the awful news had preceded me. I slumped into a seat and spoke to no one.

Reaching home, I raced into the house, changed out of school clothes, and fled to the woods. My usual evening chore was to bring the cows from the field or woods for milking. That afternoon I first sought out a favorite woodland haven.

In the far corner of Father's woods stood a maple tree, its gnarled limbs and low branches nudging the grass below. Often I had poured out my little-girl troubles to that friendly tree, but this time I carried a burden far too big for a tree. Miserable and dejected, I felt wicked and desperately alone. Leaving the old tree and ducking into a nearby grove of quaking aspen, I knelt. That spot became an altar, for there I confessed my terrible guilt to God and felt his forgiveness flood my heart.

Years passed before I understood what transpired that autumn afternoon. The man in Jesus' parable cried, "God, be merciful to me, a sinner." My childish words were different, but I made the same request. To me the heavenly Father dispensed mercy every bit as freely as He did to that repentant tax collector.

I returned to the old tree and flung myself on the ground, sobbing. Much later I heard my brother calling the cows. The dim, rhythmical tinkle of bells followed as the beasts, heavy with milk, lumbered up the lane. As the sun sank low in the west, I got up and started home.

I could face the family now, and returning to school the next day no longer seemed impossible. Never, never again would I be so devastatingly, totally alone. I had found the "Friend that sticketh closer than a brother." ■

BROOKHAVEN
WESLEYAN CHURCH
2960 E. 38th & Garthwaite
Marion, Indiana 46952

෩3ൟ

Moment of Promise

God used an eighth-grade essay assignment to help me break free from crippling insecurity.

Our teacher instructed us to compose a "Career Book," with a chapter for each career we had ever thought of pursuing. As she explained what to do, visions of homemaker, candy-store clerk, seamstress, teacher, and artist all danced before me. *Yes,* I concluded, *I'll like this project.* Then I remembered events of an extraordinary summer evening. The memory had lain in my heart undisclosed but very much alive. I wondered how I could describe the experience, afraid that others would laugh if I shared it.

The matter troubled me for days. *Maybe I can just leave it out of my story,* I thought. *No one will know.* But in the end I knew the concluding chapter of my Career Book must be titled, "Missionary."

A fire that destroyed our old home also burned up that composition book. But this is the story it told:

The summer I was ten, a traveling evangelist held tent meetings about a mile from our home. Neighbors frequently took us children to the services. I do not remember much of what the evangelist said, but I realized that he had answers to some of the things that had troubled me for a long time. He talked of the God who was not "Something or Someone Out There," unknowable and unreachable. He was the true God, who had reached out to us by giving His Son, Jesus Christ, to die on a cross for our sins. Not only so, but Jesus had risen from the dead and promised to come again to take all who have trusted in Him to be with Him forever.

Because I wanted to know more, I was bitterly disappointed one evening when Father did not allow me to go to the meeting. I went to my room crying. Later hearing singing, I sat up to catch the distant strains. At the same moment a soft glow filtered into the room. Ever so clearly, I heard these words: "Mary, will you be a missionary for Me?"

"Yes, Lord," I whispered.

The music ceased. The glow faded. Alarmed, I ran down the hall to my brother Orville's room. Startled by the intrusion, he asked me what was the matter.

"Did you hear anything?" I asked.

"No," he replied sleepily.

"Any music?" I questioned.

"No-o-o!" he mumbled, then as an afterthought said, "Oh, maybe it was the neighbor's radio."

I did not correct him. Nor did I explain why I had come or what I had seen and heard. After a while I went back to my room, but not to sleep. All was dark and quiet. I lay for a long time thinking on the unusual happenings. The music could have come from the tent meeting; sounds carry far on quiet summer evenings. The light might have been an afterglow of departing sunlight reflecting off a cloud. But the voice had been so clear, so near, so real—it had to be from God.

My "yes" to that voice was the promise that set the course of my life.

As with most homework, when I finished my composition, I gave it to Mother for checking. The following morning I found the meticulously corrected work lying on a stack of materials ready for school. The school bus was due and the house buzzed as Mother came in from chores. She made no comment about what I had written. Several years passed before she did.

About that time the Great Depression slammed into America, knocking the country off its economic feet for nearly all of the 1930s. It profoundly affected my teen-age years. Shortly before the Wall

Street crash, Father mortgaged the farm to build a new barn and remodel our house. That mortgage put great pressure on family resources.

As part of a family working to save our home and farm from bankruptcy, I had little time or money to engage in normal activities of young people. I complained. Thoughtlessly I fussed about plain meals and monotonous school lunches. I did not appreciate the well-made dresses Mother and my sister Ruth sewed for me, but sighed for store-bought clothes. I begged for a new coat instead of hand-me-downs, blind to the fact that Mother's only coat was a threadbare, lightweight jacket.

In spite of my complaining attitude, those years of close-to-the-ground living taught me that no field or garden yields a harvest without long months of fatiguing and often heart-breaking labor. It was a lesson I would need for the future.

The most severe economic strains for our family ended before I finished high school. I wanted to go right on to further education. But Father insisted his girls first gain experience outside our home, and my parents found live-in employment for me with a family who had five small children.

The Depression had depleted Mother's physical resources. That autumn she entered a tuberculosis sanitarium. Rest and nourishing food, the only treatment then available, brought back some strength. Over all, however, she continued to decline.

The following summer doctors allowed Mother to come home for a few weeks. I remember well a special day alone with her, though I thoughtlessly fatigued her with my ceaseless chit-chat. In the course of that chatter, I talked about a model home I had recently seen and said, "I'd like one like that some day."

Mother's response surprised me: "No, Mary, you're not going to have a house like that. You're going to have a little grass hut down in South America." It was the only time she ever alluded to what she had read in my Career Book. Three mornings later they came to tell me she had slipped away during the night.

At nineteen I wished for more years with Mother. But I am grateful for that last day together. To know that she remembered my promise and believed that one day I would fulfill it greatly encouraged me. ■

❧4❧
Surprising Promise

As a wise father had known, my two years as housemaid provided invaluable experience. I learned how it felt to receive orders and correction—also the importance of encouragement from an employer.

As Father was not yet able to finance an education for me in the field of microbiology, he encouraged me to consider nursing instead. Doing so, I applied and was accepted for training at the Methodist Hospital School of Nursing in Indianapolis.

I found nurse training rigorous and exacting, and at the same time rewarding. With new friends I studied, worked, laughed and cried.

The first year of training I searched for a church that "fit." As the pressure of work and study crowded in, the search lapsed. Occasionally, though, as duties permitted, I joined in Youth for Christ rallies and Nurses Christian Fellowship meetings.

During my second year a friend invited me to a church that stirred memories of those earlier tent meetings. After a hearty hymn or two, the pastor called for testimonies, and I began to feel ill at ease. But, seated in the middle of a pew near the front of the church, I could not gracefully escape. I tried to close my mind and ears—until the words of a young student arrested my attention. "I'm thankful to know Jesus as my personal Savior," he said earnestly, relating how God had helped him that very day at school. "I'm glad I have eternal life," he concluded, "and am God's child forever."

Presumption! I thought, refusing to believe in the possibility of such a relationship with the God of the universe. Yet deep in my heart I wished it could be so.

Some months later an upper-classman invited me to a Bible conference. Though I did not know what to expect, I agreed to go. That week, under the ministry of Dr. H. A. Ironside, dormant seeds in my heart began to sprout and mature.

I had tried to do what I thought God expected of me in order to gain His favor. Now I learned that salvation from sin and the power to live a spiritual life came not by "doing," but simply by trusting in what Jesus Christ had already done for me. My Bible took on meaning, and prayer came alive as I talked to *my* heavenly Father.

I began to grasp the significance of those earlier experiences. God had used the out-of-the-ordinary call to the mission field to keep me through unpredictable teen-age years when I had no real compass. I realized that my spiritual birthday was indeed that memorable day alone in the woods when I confessed the sin of my heart and found forgiveness and acceptance with God. But without the nourishment of God's Word, I had not grown.

Two verses a faithful counselor gave me anchored my faith—John 1:12: "As many as received him (Jesus), to them gave he power to become the sons of God, even to them that believe on his name;" and John 3:36: "He that believeth on the Son hath everlasting life; and he that believeth not the Son shall not see life, but the wrath of God abideth on him" (KJV). Later, encouraged to select a "life verse," I chose 2 Corinthians 5:21: "For he [God] hath made him [Christ] to be sin for us, who knew no sin, that we might be made the righteousness of God in him" (KJV).

Nurse's training matured me. Study, work, and fun outings with friends restored my confidence. Personal Bible study, regular teaching from God's Word, and Christian fellowship encouraged my walk with the Lord. When I no longer hesitated to acknowledge His hand on me, commitment to the promise I had made to be a missionary deepened.

When Father came for my baccalaureate and graduation, I told him of my plans for missionary training. He expressed strong disapproval and insisted I return home for a few days before taking further action.

During the stressful weekend that followed Father

broached the matter of further study by asking about my former interest in microbiology. "That's a coming field, you know," he said, "with a good future and money. If you will forget this idea of being a missionary, I'll put you through university with all your fees paid—*and* you will not need to pay me back."

Father's words astounded me. Afraid I would cry if I tried to reply, I sat quietly for a few minutes, then shook my head. Again he urged me to consider his generous offer.

I stood to go and through tears said, "Dad, this desire to be a missionary is not something urged upon me by friends. I have known for years, even before I went into nursing, that this is what I am to do."

I turned toward the stairs. Calling me back, Father reached into the magazine rack beside his chair. Drawing out two catalogs, he held them out to me. "I wonder if you have considered all the options, Mary," he said quietly. On the catalog covers I saw the names, "Columbia University" and "Moody Bible Institute."

My head and my heart whirled as I took the books and climbed the steps. Sleep did not come easily that night. I realized how inconsiderate I had been in not telling Father earlier about my missionary call. Unlike Mother, he had never read my "Career Book."

The nine-mile drive back to the bus the next morning passed too quietly. Though Father had given interest-free loans to each of us girls for education, we knew they were loans. I had to repay my nursing-school debt before I could consider going on to further education. Returning to Indianapolis, I canceled my application to seminary and accepted a position in a small county hospital. Living frugally, I was debt-free in ten months.

With my debt paid and State Board Exams for nursing accreditation behind me, I again applied for missionary training. Only a few days later, however, my family summoned me home to care for Father, who had sustained a nasty back injury in a farm accident. I went with some apprehension.

One evening after I had settled in at home again, I took my dinner to my father's room so that Dad and I could eat together. When he asked about my plans, I told him I had applied to a Bible school. Though I sensed no disapproval, he asked how I planned to pay tuition and fees, knowing I could have saved little as I had just finished repaying him.

"I will work and study at the same time," I replied.

In response Father offered financial help if I needed it. As much as I appreciated his offer, I felt I should decline. I had just begun to take my first baby steps of faith, and I needed to learn complete dependence on my heavenly Father.

When Dad improved, I returned to my job. After I completed my one-year contract, a friend and I bravely boarded the train for Philadelphia to begin a new adventure in learning. We arrived with little money or wisdom, but a growing faith.

For three years the heavenly Husbandman cultivated me at the Philadelphia School of Bible on Spring Garden Street—and not only in the area of

Bible training, but in nursing. My first year I worked as assistant school nurse. The second and third years I was charge nurse, with my friend as assistant. We shared the challenging duties and decisions while carrying the full study program. On alternate weekends and holidays we often did off-campus private-duty nursing.

At daily chapel, as speakers presented needs from every part of the world, I wondered where I might help lift a load. The last year of Bible school I prayed specifically that God would show me by directing me to the mission organization with which He would have me work.

The Lord's guidance came one snowy Sunday in December. Several of us went to the church that a favorite professor pastored. Three people of the China Inland Mission shared the challenging service. As they spoke, the Lord gave a quiet, yet deep assurance that CIM was His choice for me.

With others from the Asia Prayer Band, I began going to weekly prayer meetings at CIM's North American headquarters in suburban Philadelphia. The welcome we received at the end of our long subway and streetcar ride made the effort worthwhile. Those prayer times throbbed with life. Through them the Lord taught me to pray and to care deeply for China.

Twelve days after graduating from Bible school, I entered the mission's summer candidate program. Ten weeks later, along with fifteen others, I emerged a probationary member. We had studied the history, geography, religions, and culture of China, as well as the history and distinctives of the eighty-two-year-old mission. Those studies revealed the deep commitment of the founder and early pioneers. I saw a similar commitment in the lives of our missionary teachers. Outside of class they playfully bantered in Chinese, revealing an obvious love for the language. I wondered if I could ever learn such strange words!

Two texts written in bold, flowing Chinese characters on twin silk scrolls on the living room wall ministered deep assurance to me. They were the mission's mottoes: *Ebenezer* and *Jehovah Jireh*. In English they mean, "Hitherto hath the Lord helped us," and "The Lord will provide." At daily prayer times, though a large map of China was pulled down from a case near the ceiling and covered the two scrolls, it seemed as if I could still see those promises of Scripture shining through. They were potent, reassuring pledges of God's enabling and faithfulness.

On leaving candidate school, each new worker carried a thick Chinese/English dictionary and a list of the 214 radicals which, in different combinations, make up all Chinese characters. These we had to learn on our voyage to China! We also took with us an "outfit list," a sheaf of typewritten pages listing all of the items we would need for the anticipated seven years in China. A final look into the faces of our mentors as we said goodbye helped ease fears of the unknown. They had gone this way before us; we knew they would pray.

I took the overnight train home to Indiana to prepare to sail in five weeks. The fact that our shipping cases and trunks had to be at the San Francisco dock a week before we sailed meant that we had only four weeks to collect and pack for the years ahead. In the days that followed I lived an adventure in buying, sewing, labeling, packing and freighting items from that incredible outfit list.

Though most of those hectic weeks blur together, my memory of the last Sunday at home will always remain special. Father accepted an invitation to a farewell program at the neighborhood church I had attended as a child.

Following the dinner and program, Father and I drove home. As I reached for the handle to open the car door, Father said, "Mary, there's something I want to tell you."

I waited for him to continue.

"When your mother and I were first married, before any of you children came, we pledged one of you to God for special service." With great feeling he added, "I guess you're the one."

Utterly surprised, I struggled to sort out my thoughts and emotions. Flashbacks stirred memories of times I had taken offense at Father's efforts to direct me. Now I saw that his seeming disapproval had in reality been his way of making me certain of the path I chose. With wonder I realized that God's direction for my life had been set in motion long before that night I sat at home, not allowed to attend the tent meeting. Instead it had been when a young bride and groom promised one of their unborn offspring to God for His service. ■

ಐ5ಐ

Westward to the East

When it came time for me to leave home for China, Father drove me, without fanfare, to the local train depot.

Subdued, however, hardly described my send-off from Colorado, where I had stopped to see a newborn niece. I had reservations out of Denver on the last train that could get me to the West Coast before our ship sailed. Therein lurked disaster.

On departure day, with my bags packed into my brother-in-law's car, we had just turned from the driveway when our farewellers shouted, "Stop! You have a flat tire!"

We hastily reloaded the baggage into a neighbor's car and again started on our way. Several miles on, in a residential part of the city, the borrowed car also developed a flat! Remembering a filling station a few blocks back, my brother-in-law set off on the run for assistance. I fidgeted with my watch. He returned

with the owner of the gas station, having persuaded
him to close up shop and drive us to the train station.

Again we frantically transferred bags. Anxious now
about the train's imminent departure, we urged our
good-hearted chauffeur to hurry. But each time he
tried to go faster, the wheels of the old car shimmied
hopelessly.

We crept up to the cavernous train station right at
departure time. Grabbing my assorted baggage, we
raced toward the already-moving San Francisco Express. As the train gathered speed, I leaped from the
level platform onto the next-to-the-last coach. A
breathless brother-in-law threw my heavy bags in
behind me. Tearfully I collapsed into an empty seat.
Before long, a kindly porter, who had witnessed our
wild race, came to show me to my berth several cars
forward.

The train climbed quickly into snow-whitened

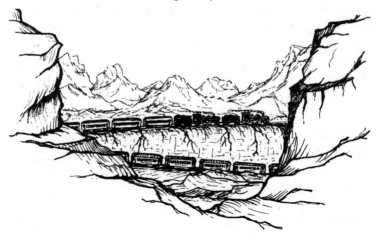

mountains. As we wound our way past craggy peaks, aglow, first in the setting sun, later in brilliant moon-light, I relaxed, enjoying my first unhurried hours in weeks. Though I wanted to stay awake to watch the changing views, I soon succumbed to sleep.

The next day we sped through Utah's flat salt lands. By evening we were again ascending into high mountains. Awed by their grandeur and beauty, I was reminded that the One who created those towering citadels loved and cared for me.

Three days out of Denver, we rolled into California's lush valleys and rumbled on to the city of San Francisco.

The following afternoon, October 3, 1947, our party boarded the *Marine Adder,* a converted troop ship on which we would sail nearly half way around the world. A porthole-less cabin with four triple-deck bunks housed eleven of us for the next 24 days. For reasons soon obvious, we dubbed our ship *"The Marine Odor."*

Scarcely beyond San Francisco's Golden Gate Bridge I began to wonder why I had ever wanted to see some really big waves. I was a poor sailor.

I found much to delight, however. The sea and sky changed moods constantly. The sun, moon, and stars had never looked so bright. Sea creatures entertained us with their antics as they played in the wake of our ship or tussled with scraps of food tossed overboard.

As my woozy head allowed, I tried to learn those puzzling Chinese radicals given us when we left candidate school, but with scant success. I joined others for daily prayer and Bible study, wrote letters, helped entertain children. When the sea was calm, I entered into games on deck.

At times I searched out a quiet corner where, with a visor pulled well over my eyes, I spent time alone. I needed those hours with the Lord, both for day-by-day living on shipboard and as preparation for the totally new life that awaited.

First the Hawaiian Islands, then the Philippines, and finally the continent of Asia rose out of the sea.

On our last day at sea, we steamed into waters muddied by China's mighty Yangtze River. The sea lay glassy calm that evening, glowing in the sunset. I stayed on deck until the coastline merged into sea and sky. *What will China hold for me?* I wondered. *What will I be able to give to her? Will some of her people come to know the Savior because I have come?*

Near noon the following day we docked in Shanghai's teeming port amid the confusion of thronging passengers, welcoming relatives, and the clamor of porters and coolies. Family-like, mission personnel welcomed us and led us capably through immigration, immunizations, and customs.

Arrival formalities completed, we gathered up our hand luggage and climbed into the back of an open truck. Laughing and waving to friendly pedestrians who smiled up at us, we honked our way through choked lanes and broad boulevards to our mission's international headquarters, there to await transportation inland to language school.

For our eleven days in Shanghai the unaccustomed beset us on every hand. In the mission home I puzzled over hard-to-understand dialects of *English*. Fellow international missionaries doubtless struggled to make out mine! In the dining hall some used knives to push food onto the backs of their forks, while we Americans switched forks from hand to hand in order to pick up a knife to cut our food, then lay it down to eat from the "right" side of the fork. Chinese was not the only culture to which we would need to adapt!

Mission directors interviewed us. Their wives kindly invited us to tea. Other senior workers escorted us to cloth shops, where we stared wide-eyed at exquisite fabrics. Going through the local bargaining ritual, our escorts bought plain cloth with wildly inflated currency. We then took our new fabric to tailor shops to be sewn into ankle-length quilted Chinese gowns.

At daily prayer meetings we learned more about China's real situation. The threatening crisis of a communist takeover had implications both for national believers and for us.

Concern, therefore, tinged our eagerness to head for language school in Angking. Twice the office booked passage on Yangtze River steamers for us, and twice the military commandeered the boats. In the end we traveled by train as far as Nanking (then the capital of China), where upriver passenger boats were less subject to diversion.

My first glimpse of China beyond Shanghai came through the open windows of our crowded coach. When we pulled out of Shanghai's central station, every car on the train seemed filled to capacity. Yet at every sub-station more people, seeking safety in the countryside, scrambled on. Aisles and every other bit of floor space filled until we hardly had a place to put our feet. Once outside the city and police control, people clambered onto the tops of the coaches and sat on their baskets or rolled-up bedding.

Mid-afternoon we reached Nanking and went directly to the river to find the launch booked for us. We had thought our trans-Pacific quarters cramped! They were luxury by comparison to the *five-and-a-half-foot-square* cabin four of us now shared. A stool and three bare-board bunks comprised the room's only furnishings. I slept on the floor. Each night I zipped my sleeping bag securely shut and hoped, *in vain*, to keep little creatures from sharing my comforts! Day and night curious fellow passengers peered through our two barred windows, watching our every movement and effectively shutting out fresh air.

The first two nights our little steamer docked at cities where fellow missionaries lived. Advised of our coming, they invited us to their homes for evening meals. How good it felt to escape the confines of our limited quarters for even those few hours! Apart from those evenings, we didn't leave our cabin for three and a half days.

That little square of space had to serve as living room, dining room, bedroom and bathroom all in one.

Each morning a container of wash water was delivered to our cabin. Mid-morning and mid-afternoon a worker from the galley brought a wooden bucket of boiled or steamed rice, along with a bowl of hot soup or fried vegetables. Seasoned male missionary escorts slept on the crowded deck outside our door and accepted our shyly passed refuse to be emptied overboard.

We anchored midstream the third night. The following afternoon we reached Anking, where we would study Chinese. With joy we climbed ashore. Competent Chinese helpers from the language school took charge of our bags, carrying them to the school compound suspended from the ends of shoulder poles or in squeaking wheelbarrows. Gleeful children danced about us, laughing and pointing at our strange clothes, shoes, hats, hair, and noses as we picked our way along narrow lanes and past open-fronted shops to the gate of the Gospel Hall. Behind the church stood our language school.

My desire to respond to words and looks of inquiry had grown perceptibly during those travel days. Able only to nod and smile— possibly at the wrong time—I felt ready to tackle language learning in earnest. ■

℘6℘

So Much to Learn!

*T*hough impatient to get to language study, we needed to wait for fellow students still held up in Shanghai. The delay gave time to settle into new surroundings and rout from bedding, clothing, and hair some of the unwelcome creatures we had collected on our river trip.

School routines began as soon as the later group arrived. At six each morning the gardener jolted us awake by furiously beating a large brass gong as he went from building to building. He must have smiled to himself, envisioning the stir he created within! Our days ended with the soft whir of the class buzzer at ten.

With innocent optimism I began the study of Chinese. Before many days, however, I was dismayed at the incredible difference between the sounds my teacher made as he spoke and those coming from my mouth! I stumbled over turned-around grammar and

staggered at the strange script. Old feelings of inadequacy surfaced.

After a month the superintendent divided our class
of fifty-two into two groups—quicker learners in one
and slower learners in the other. In making the assignments—me to the slower group—he urged all of us to
guard our personal Bible study and prayer times,
concluding, "Those who pray the most will get the
language the quickest."

Taking his words seriously, I rose at five-thirty and
then at five o'clock. In my dark, chilly room I hastened
through a sponge bath in water poured from the hot
water bottle I had taken into my sleeping bag the
night before. After dressing in multiple layers of clothing, I hurried along the dark hall to the outside toilet.
When I returned, mine was still the only light. *I shall
do all right now*, I thought. But when I began compar-
ing myself to others, Bible study grew tedious and
prayer barren—and I remained near the bottom of the
class.

Our regular afternoon volleyball games, monthly
birthday celebrations, and multi-national festivities
lightened the long hours of study. During those infor-
mal times I came to know and appreciate my fellow
students. They came from Switzerland, Finland, Nor-
way, Sweden, Denmark, New Zealand, Australia, England, Scotland, Canada, and the United States. We
seemed most closely drawn together in our evening
"China Prayer Time," when intercessors often prayed
in their mother tongues.

Some weekends our mentors took us to quaint

shops in the city or for walks outside the old city wall. We went in small groups to create less of a stir. Often on such outings we saw battalions of youthful soldiers, some suffering rasping coughs, as they trudged along the muddy roads with only straw sandals on their feet. Perspiring with strain, even in the damp chill, they bent beneath loads of heavy equipment strapped on their backs or swinging from carrying poles.

Sundays we went to the Gospel Chapel, again in small groups. As the people gathered sang, prayed, and preached, I strained to catch familiar words in Chinese.

Winter winds penetrated our quarters. Stoves took the chill off common rooms, but not from the bedrooms. New missionaries with kerosene heaters were asked not to use them. Fuel oil was scarce and expensive in war-torn China; such "waste" would be misunderstood. Instead, we were introduced to the common earthenware braziers that held pieces of live charcoal buried in layers of ash. These warmed our feet, but not our cold noses!

I rejoiced when spring arrived. Walks past country homes, now surrounded by flowering fruit trees and newly planted gardens, revived my sagging spirit. Laughing children played about us as we gathered wild flowers. When they responded to some of my simple questions, I exulted. *Maybe I can get this language after all!* I thought.

But back at school I wallowed in self-pity as others surged ahead—mastering tones, vocabulary, and phrases.

*F*ew of us knew the kind of work we would do or
to what part of China we would be assigned. Our
hopes and fears focused on "designation day" set in
April, when a mission director would come for interviews and make appointments.

For months I had followed with prayerful interest a
developing medical work among an unreached people
group near the border of Tibet. Challenged by the
need, I wondered if I might be assigned there.

With interviews scheduled alphabetically, I was not
called until the third afternoon. The director, a saintly
English gentleman named John Sinton, had a pleasant,
relaxed manner. After prayer, his first question was to
the point: "Mary, how would you like to join the
medical team to work among the Nosu people on the
borders of Tibet?"

I thought my heart would burst! After my enthusiastic "I would!" we prayed together about the new
work and discussed where I could go to continue
Chinese language study before heading to Nosuland.

As my initial euphoria faded, gnawing fears crept
in. *That will mean learning another language! Can I do
that?* I fretted. *At the rate I'm learning Chinese that will
take years! I will have forgotten all of my nursing by then!*

I knew God's promises. Nor could I forget the
promise I had made. Still questions persisted.

I hesitated, not as a conscious decision to manage
my own life, but from habit. I excused myself with,
Well, I can't help it. After all, I'm only human! I had yet to
learn that submission to God's will is essential in
service for Him. Defeats and frustrations continued

until the One who could help me got my reluctant attention.

Only those of us in the second stream remained at the language school when word came to be ready to leave at a moment's notice. As the rumble of distant shelling and occasional gunfire nearby kept us aware of our precarious situation, the order to evacuate hardly came as a surprise.

The next morning our school exploded with feverish bustle. Throughout the day, carriers ferried baggage and school equipment to the riverside. The old school would never again see such activity; we would be the last trainees to pass through those familiar halls.

After an early supper we said regretful goodbyes to the household staff, who had so kindly and efficiently cared for us. They, our teachers, and the brothers and sisters at the chapel had been our first Chinese friends.

At twilight we made our way through the city's lanes for the last time. At the wharf we found our gear already loaded on the boat. Though less crowded than the ride to Anking, available space was still at a premium. With others, I took my sleeping bag to the flat roof over the pilot's cabin.

Throughout the night, boats anchored beside us danced and bobbed in the swiftly flowing waters. Half a block away the city's old pagoda, with a single tiny light glowing at its top, towered above us. A half moon darted in and out of flying clouds.

I had just dozed off when a brilliantly lit luxury liner drew in for the night. As raucous music drowned out the peaceful croaking of frogs, I pulled the hood of my sleeping bag over my head.

An early morning blast from our boat's steam whistle and a shower of cinders signaled our departure. We lurched from the mooring. Awakened, I watched the zigzag wake we made and felt a certain nostalgia as the first rays of the sun peeped over receding housetops.

At first we churned through lowlands, passing lone thatched cottages standing in fields of grain or houses clustered at the river's edge. Midmorning we steamed into hill country. Low foothills stretched away to purple mountains that rose higher and higher in the distance. Throughout the day we met or passed hundreds of boats on the broad river.

Sunset brought us to a city famed for fine china and porcelain. We spent the night in a missionary guest house. At dawn we scrambled from our sleeping bags in response to shouts that all baggage must be ready to go in ten minutes. Once the baggage had gone, we walked to a nearby restaurant for a breakfast of glutinous rice, hard-fried eggs, boiled cabbage, and a stir-fry of beef and vegetables. Well fortified, we returned to the guest house, where we learned the reason for our hasty departure from language school in Anking. We were going to the top of Kuling Mountain to possess premises the mission had recently acquired.

We climbed into the back of an open truck for our first motor ride since Shanghai. The bumpy twelve-mile trip took us to the foot of the mountain to begin our ascent on foot. For hours, then, we scrambled over rugged terrain and forced ourselves to continue up hundreds of steep steps carved into the mountainside.

Luxuriant jungle growth covered all but rocky out-croppings. Pink and white wild roses and brilliant azaleas grew in profusion; waterfalls abounded. The air cooled quickly as we climbed. At times we rounded a sharp curve to see checkerboard fields on the broad plains far below. People hurrying to tasks looked like tiny ants in the shimmering distance. *Did they know about Jesus?* I wondered. *And what about the friendly folk toiling along the paths we had just traversed?*

Fairy Glen Hotel, our new home, exceeded our wildest imaginations. We could never have dreamed that such a place, on a mountaintop in Central China, would be the site for our continuing language learn-ing. Only seven days prior to our arrival the owners of that fabulous establishment, aware of China's rapidly deteriorating political climate, sold the hotel with all its contents to our mission *for one U.S. dollar!*

For a week we assisted with hotel inventory before buckling down to study in unbelievably opulent sur-roundings.

The break had done me good. I pressed on to the written and oral exams. Walks at end of day through luxuriant gardens stimulated and renewed me.

*E*vening walks frequently took us down a short, wooded path to our mission's temporary primary school. A yearly sports day there, celebrating the founding of the original Chefoo school, provided the occasion for God to get through to me about my growing attitude of self-reliance.

We language students were not only invited to watch the sports events, but to participate. Organizers asked me to be on the softball team. I was delighted and looked forward to playing. I thought—though I would never have said it aloud—*I may not be good at this language, but I'll show them I can play softball!*

Though too many players had been asked for our team, I did not relinquish my place. At the start of the game I struck a ball and scrambled safely to first base. A teammate followed with a home run. Running ahead of him on perfectly smooth turf, I collapsed on the ground, my right foot fractured.

A thought exploded in my head: *You were going to show you could play ball, were you?* I sat out the game. Later teammates carried me back to the hotel.

Others may not have known what God was doing in my life, but I knew He had touched my foot as He had touched Jacob's thigh many centuries before. *Will I*, I wondered, *because of pride, be a cripple like Jacob the rest of my life?*

For months God had been trying to get my attention. In the pressure to complete exams, I had not heard Him out. He now had my full attention! ■

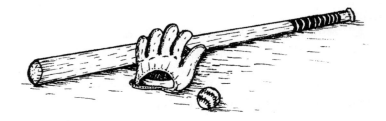

☜7☞
Promise Rekindled

Having completed the first section of our Chinese language course, four of us new missionaries left our mountaintop accommodations to travel together to Chungking in west China.

Still on crutches, I had to ride down the mountain in a hammock-like chair, suspended between poles that rested on the shoulders of eight carriers. The descent had me cringing, especially down one flight of a thousand continuous steps. But even that ride paled beside the spine-tingling flight across China's rugged heartland in a battered, twenty-one-passenger twin-engine Sky-Master. Because we arrived at the Chungking airport ahead of the telegram sent two days earlier, no one met us. Kindly, a Chinese fellow-passenger helped us find our way.

The room I shared on the top floor of the mission home had a commanding view of the city. Between crowded tin and tile roofs below, I saw rich and poor

going about their daily tasks. Beyond the houses the
Yangtze flowed, alive with river traffic as it hustled
eastward to the Pacific Ocean nearly three thousand
miles away.

A student from the nearby Bible seminary had been
asked to help me make the necessary changes from
standard Chinese to the west Sichuan dialect. One
morning I found her waiting as I returned from sham-
pooing my hair. "Sorry to keep you waiting," I meant
to apologize, "I've just washed my hair."

For a moment the young woman stared dumbly at
my tousled head, then fell back on my bed convulsed
with laughter. Instead of the word for human hair, I
had used the word for horse hair or feathers! I joined
her laughter, though soberly I wondered if I would
ever learn to speak Chinese correctly.

When the summer heat and humidity in the river
valley grew oppressive, we students shifted to
a vacation bungalow in the hills beyond the river.

I had just gone through a year of continual change,
each change carrying its particular kind of stress. Now
in a vacation atmosphere, I found it impossible to
maintain the required hours of daily study. Because
my foot still pained me as I hobbled about, I felt
hemmed in. I longed to roam the hills and to communicate in the new language. Disturbing thoughts
crowded my mind: *I'll never make a missionary! Why am
I here? It would be better to go home now rather than waste
more of my time and the mission's money.*

The next moment I wanted with all my heart to

remain. The duel raged. Sharing my anxiety with vacationing senior workers helped. They under-stood—they had traveled this road before me.

In the end, a series of messages at a summer Bible conference put the spotlight on the real problem. As the conference speaker emphasized the need to die to self, I resisted giving up the control of my life. Violent storms erupted in my heart. God's Spirit probed for roots of self and pride. Finally my defenses crumbled, and I confessed to Him my sinful attitudes.

Humbled by His righteous judgment and warmed by His fathomless love, I rekindled my promise and found the courage to continue.

I came to understand more fully the words which the Apostle Paul wrote to the Christians at Philippi: "Be careful for nothing, but in everything by prayer and supplication, *with thanksgiving,* let your requests be made known unto God, and the peace of God which passeth all understanding shall keep your hearts and minds through Christ Jesus" (Ph. 4:6, 7, KJV).

Is giving thanks in the middle of life's difficult situations really God's way to free me from anxiety and to have peace? I wondered.

I chose to accept what God had said and found that thanksgiving unlocked doors that anxiety had closed. I called this truth my "thanksgiving key." Learning how and when to use the key took diligence.

Toward the end of summer I was invited to lead morning devotions with the domestic staff. I prac-

ticed my carefully written-out message on any senior
missionary I could badger into listening. It took about
three minutes! The Chinese workers, who had listened to many a new missionary's first stumbling
effort, kindly declared they understood. They were
generous. Probably they had heard the Zacchaeus
story so many times that they knew what *should* be
said!

By the end of August the days turned hot even in
the hills. Rice in the terraced fields changed from lush
green to copper brown. Many evenings students and
guests sat outside under starlit skies to catch a breeze
and to watch the lights of Chungking city come on
and begin to twinkle in the darkness below. Most
often those pleasant evenings ended in spontaneous
praise, singing, and prayer.

When time came to close the vacation bungalow
for the season, I felt a certain sadness. God had
done a deep work in my life during those weeks, and
I was truly grateful.

My foot now nearly healed, I walked with others
down to the city. What I saw that morning made me
aware of how little I knew the real China. Beside the
narrow footpaths, tiny piles of ash grew larger beneath sticks of smoldering incense, placed there to
implore the gods to withhold the rains until rice could
be harvested.

By midday we reached the river. While we waited
for a ferry to cross, I witnessed a sight I shall never
forget. From the corner of my eye I noticed people

stepping around something. Looking closer, I saw a man, wild-eyed with fear and struggling to breathe, lying at the water's edge. The crowds hurried by. No one offered to help or seemed disturbed by his plight. I caught the words, "beggar" or "criminal" from some who saw my dismay.

It may be so, I thought, *but he, too, is a person with a soul.*

The ferry came; the crowd surged forward. Someone called my name, and I, too, passed by. Numbly I gripped the handrail and agonized as the distance widened between us and the dying man, now alone on the sand. I wondered how soon encroaching waters would wash his body away. In my heart I cried, *When, Lord, will I be able to help folks like that?*

A few weeks later on a cool autumn evening five of us bound for my first inland home boarded a small upriver steamer. We held tickets for cabins, but we found all cabins occupied. The cheerful captain assured us there would be accommodations when those who had come to see friends off left the boat. We huddled together on the windy prow, waiting for an exodus that never came.

Around midnight, thoroughly chilled and weary, we followed others down a rope ladder to a more sheltered spot on the pontoon to which we were anchored. We four women snuggled together in two sleeping bags and tried to rest. Our male escort, for warmth, sat with his back hunched against the side of a grunting hog securely tied in a long wicker basket.

Along with several other hogs, it would be loaded into the hold for transport the next morning.

Before dawn we clambered back onto the boat to look for the promised cabin. The cabins had been overbooked. The pilot pushed some sleeping bodies closer together to make room for us to sit in front of his cabin. While the space did not allow us to lie down, we appreciated the wall as a backrest.

Developing a nasty cold, I let misery engulf me. Romantic ideas of missionary life and travel began to fade! A long day followed.

That night we anchored beside a small freighter. Our escort persuaded the owner to let us sleep on his small craft. As rough and uneven as the floor was, we enjoyed the luxury of just stretching out.

A second weary day of travel followed. That evening we again hoped for a place to lie flat. When the anchor went down midstream, our hopes sank with it.

Seeing others making for the roof, we ventured after them. We found a vacant space near the center of the slanting roof and rigged up a flannel sheet above us. Securing one end of our canopy to the smoke stack, we guiltily tied the other to a sign that read, "Unauthorized persons not allowed on the roof." Though we did wonder if anyone had ever fallen off the roof in his sleep, we rested there until morning. Just as day broke, the crew stoked up the boilers. Within seconds, fine black soot floated down upon us. We grabbed our rapidly graying bedding and fled below.

On our third day of travel the boat crept along as it maneuvered through fog and treacherous rapids in the increasingly shallow water. I have seldom heard sweeter words than, "Next stop, Luhsien!"

During the trip I had tried (but without great success) to use my "thanksgiving key." Now at our new home some simple medicines, a bath, and a light supper made it easier. When finally led to a warm bed piled with soft blankets, the key turned easily. Before drifting off to sleep in that cozy bed, I wondered if I would ever learn to use that key in the middle of difficult situations. The years ahead would give ample opportunities to find out. ∎

Old China

Adapted from the inside cover of the book,
Strong Tower, by A. J. Broomhall,
published by the China Inland Mission
in London in 1947

0   500   1000   1500

Scale of Miles

Teacher Ho

My new mission family, senior workers Ron and Gwen Roberts and two single workers, jolly Mildred Schroder and reserved Dorothy North, were all Australian. Studious Pearl McCullough and I, the newcomers, added Irish and American flavors to the household.

Others on the compound soon became family too. The most senior staff member was Teacher Ho, a gracious and tireless worker among women and children. We lovingly called her Ho-Ho. Philip, a keen young Chinese pastor from eastern China, and Andrew, his local assistant, directed ministry to the adult congregation. An elderly widowed vegetable seller who lived next to Teacher Ho's kitchen, though not a staff member, gave invaluable support to the ministry. We called her Anna because, like the Anna in Luke 2, she served God faithfully by fasting and prayer. The sturdy but diminutive gatekeeper and his family, along with Brother One, our cook, and Brother Two, his younger brother, serving as water carrier and gardener, completed the number of those living on the mission compound.

The church in Luhsien had grown from its beginning fifty years earlier into the hub of a county-wide outreach. Teacher Ho had labored beside many of those early pioneers. For her unassuming assistance and wise counsel, nationals and missionaries alike honored and respected her. All who knew her welcomed her into their homes. Often with a basket of eggs or fruit on her arm, she took me with her to encourage and pray with the sick, blind, or otherwise needy. From her I learned Chinese Christian ethics and etiquette.

Teacher Ho kept her silver-flecked black hair pulled tightly into a tiny bun at the nape of her neck. Sparkling eyes peered from her round and pleasant, but usually unsmiling face. A birth injury had left her with a slight limp and a left-sided weakness. She never complained, though—nor did she let the handicap prevent her from ministering to others.

From my room I often saw Ho-Ho in the shaded alley behind her home, bending over a wooden washtub doing her laundry. Across the tub, a young girl or woman would squat on a low stool, learning from the gentle teacher. Sometimes a cooing baby, wrapped in a cozy red coverlet, lay securely tied in a chair nearby. Often the student leaned toward Teacher Ho, pointing to a forgotten character in the New Testament she held in her hand. I shall never know how many illiterate women and girls learned to read over that washtub. But many who lived near Luhsien's west gate owed their prized reading ability to that serene teacher in a faded blue gown.

I learned many valuable lessons sitting in on Teacher Ho's large Sunday school class. Boys and girls listened attentively as she told Bible stories. I soon discovered that the children's good behavior reflected more than the teacher's skill in storytelling. Though she never raised her voice, I have seen her dismiss an inattentive trouble-maker. I seldom noticed the problem before she quietly advised the disruptive child to leave. The next week he usually returned to sit in the front row, where she had placed him. During the week she had visited the child's home. She never invited me along on *those* visits. She did not want the child's parents to "lose face" before a foreigner.

This no-longer-young woman helped me inestimably with language learning. She patiently corrected my improperly pronounced words and tones until I could say them accurately. Once, when I nearly cried from the effort, she asked, "Am I being too hard? Would you like me not to correct you?" If others had been as persistent, my problems would not have continued so long.

A weekday children's meeting at a soap factory a couple of miles upriver provided my earliest opportunity for regular ministry. An elder from the church, a foreman at the factory, lived there with his young family. Teacher Ho helped me prepare a simple illustration to give before she told the Bible story. That way she could unobtrusively clarify any misunderstanding my misuse of a tone or word might have caused.

If the weather was fine, we liked to walk to the factory. Little scouts usually watched for us. As we came into view, they ran toward us, shouting to their friends, "Jesus is coming! Jesus is coming!"

"May it be so!" was Teacher Ho's usual soft response before the welcoming children raced up to her. Grasping her good hand, they led us on, eager for the story time.

While participation in church services helped me develop facility in many aspects of the language, I also needed ordinary conversational Chinese. This I gained as I became better acquainted with the older Sunday school girls. Often coming to chat, they would say, "We see you just sit and look at books all day, so we've come to visit. Aren't you bored?"

Sometimes the visits were lengthy and counterproductive. If I tried to explain that I spent lots of time "looking" at books because I was learning their language, they usually responded cheerily, "Oh, we'll help you!" I found it difficult to explain that teen-age chatter didn't always help complete the material assigned for language exams. If their visits came too frequently, dear Ho-Ho would come to the rescue. Calling to my young visitors, she would ask them to run an errand or to help her with an urgent job—one she had probably just thought up!

I quickly joined the ranks of those who loved and greatly valued Teacher Ho's guidance and wisdom. ■

56

❧9❧
By-path to Tribesland

*A*s we moved into 1949, dread gripped hearts everywhere. Rumors, false and true, abounded as the jubilant, conquering communist army fanned southward and westward across the land.

Early that year our Australian seniors left for their well-earned furlough. Fred and May Purchas, an English couple with many years of experience in China, replaced them. I appreciated the Purchases' steadying influence. Many other foreign organizations were withdrawing personnel. CIM leaders felt we should remain as long as we had opportunity to encourage the church and point people to Jesus Christ. Thus the Lord gave me two more years of service—and *refining*—in Luhsien.

In those months before occupation, the devaluation of the national currency affected us more than any other hardship. Money that could purchase ten kilos of rice one day might buy only half that much a week, or even a day, later. Rice became a more stable medium of exchange. We, like our neighbors, converted our money into rice, trading it later as needed for other commodities.

Foreigners leaving west China often passed through our city. Coming to us for a place to stay, some families waited many days for transportation. Though willing to help in any way we could, prolonged stays sometimes taxed our material and emotional resources. Yet time and again we saw God's wonderful and timely provision.

Five overseas visitors stopped one night, expecting to travel on the next day. They were driving a van intended for a mission hospital several hundred miles to the north. The afternoon they arrived, a telegram came telling them to cancel their trip and return to Chungking. Funds they had in hand for their extended trip now met *our* urgent needs. Telegrams often arrived late those days, but that one came right on time!

God provided for us in many ways. Once we found a pair of gum-rubber boots in our attic that, when sold, "fed us" until a local bank had sufficient cash for money wired to us from Shanghai three weeks earlier.

When systems that once seemed normal began to crumble, bewildered people came for comfort and counsel. Night by night they crowded into the tiny street chapel to listen to messages of God's power to save from sin and to keep from despair. During those unsettling months Sunday school teachers faithfully taught the weekly Bible lessons and memory verses to scores of children and adults. On Saturdays we newer workers helped illiterate women and girls to memorize Scripture promises.

On Easter the Sunday school children repeated in unison the verses they had learned throughout the year. Proud adults beamed as they listened to the Word of God from the lips of children and grand-children.

I sensed a greater intensity at the short-term Bible school that spring. Dedicated tutors taught from God's Word doctrines that would strengthen faith, instill courage, and impart vision. Those attending wondered, sometimes aloud, "Is this our last opportunity to study together?"

I found those months a satisfyingly busy time. However, recurring bouts of malaria undermined my health. The district nurse advised me to go to a cooler climate as soon as possible. Because I could not travel alone, it looked as if I would have to wait until summer vacation time, when others headed to the mountains. Then late one evening fellow missionary Irene Cunningham, with her young son Gordon, arrived by boat from Chungking. The two had gone to the big city for the child's tonsillectomy. They planned to go on as soon as possible to their home in the mountains. Irene invited me to travel with them and spend the summer with them.

One morning, while waiting for transportation, we joined a spirited crowd at the riverside to watch the annual boat races. We mingled with the jostling crowd, chatting and giving away gospel tracts and Scripture portions. Before the final row-off our cook came looking for us, easily spotting our blond heads in the sea of dark ones. He had news that two trucks would leave for the mountains early the next morning. Immediately returning home, we packed, ate an early supper, and hurried to the river. We arrived in time to make the two-hour crossing to a village near the truck stop.

Before we disappeared into an unkept rural inn for the night, one of the drivers approached us and whispered their plans to leave before dawn. They hoped to escape unpaying passengers, whom they called "yellow fish." Often deserters from the army, these men would refuse to budge from their perches once they had climbed onto the back of a loaded vehicle.

That night an unexpected attack of malaria sent my temperature soaring. No way could we get to the medicine, packed in bags securely roped and buried in the depths of those overloaded trucks. It was a long night.

Though we left well before sunrise, we did not entirely escape the "yellow fish."

Had I not been so ill, I might have enjoyed the eleven-hour trip bouncing over the narrow road that followed a turbulent, winding river.

Nightfall brought us to the home of Walter and Helen Jespersen. Walter was the brother and uncle of my traveling companions. Though we had planned to spend one night there, I was too ill to travel on. Irene and young Gordon went on as planned to their home in the mountains. I remained behind.

Twenty-four days later the Jespersens judged me well enough to cover the last twenty-eight miles to the mountain home of the Cunninghams. Edith Jackson, a co-worker from language school who lived with the Jespersens, would accompany me.

The day we planned to go we learned that all the men who regularly carry passengers into the hills had been engaged for the funeral of a high-ranking official. As they would be unavailable for several days, someone suggested we might hire freight carriers—men who ordinarily carry coal, fuel oil, or slab salt into the mountains. "My men are reliable, honest, and do not smoke opium," boasted the manager of the carriers we hired. "They can easily get you there in a day."

We began to question such grand assurances when we saw the eight men who came to carry us and the makeshift chairs they brought for us to ride in.

We left the mission compound in pelting rain. Great drops of rain spattered right through the coarse canopy rigged over our heads.

Tiny anti-slip metal clips embedded in the carriers' straw sandals made a rhythmical sound as they trotted along. The men stopped every hour for rest and food. Around noon we turned off the narrow slab-stone road and headed up into more rugged terrain. When one of my carriers stumbled, I climbed down from the rig to give the men a break. For the first time I could see the magnificent surroundings. Not wanting to "lose face," the men urged me back into the chair. With reluctance, I returned to my skyward-only view.

By afternoon some of the men were dallying longer at each stop. The sweet smell of opium alerted us to the problem. When urged on by fellow carriers, the delayers responded with sullen looks. Knowing they could "accidentally" drop us over a cliff if they chose, we prayed earnestly for protection and safety.

Frequent forks in the now indistinct paths sparked arguments among the carriers. Twice they wanted to stop at isolated farmhouses. We urged them on. Late afternoon, as a storm gathered over distant peaks, we rounded a sharp curve and gazed across a deep, partially cultivated valley. A cluster of buildings lay on the far side. Our hearts leapt. The carriers hurried on.

Nearing the settlement, we realized we had not found our intended destination, but rather a small tribal community. As we stopped in front of the largest dwelling, the storm broke, and darkness closed us in.

Villagers quickly led us through an enclosed courtyard to shelter. The only light in the thick darkness glowed from graying embers in a fire-pit at the center of the large room. A handful of dried sticks dropped onto the smoldering ashes sent flames leaping upwards and revealed a crush of onlookers. An older woman motioned for us to shed our wet coats. Giggling girls touched our hands, felt our woolen sweaters, and pressed strands of our hair between their fingers.

When our sleeping bags appeared, brought in from the chairs on which we had ridden all day, people exclaimed in wonder. The more curious lit sticks of bamboo at the fire to examine the bags more closely. Amazement grew when we unzipped them and spread them on a wide bed to dry.

A blackened kettle set over the fire came quickly to a boil, and before long we sipped hot black tea. I doubt we could have enjoyed a meal more than we did the remnants of our crumbled lunch and that smoky mountain-brewed tea, so graciously served in tin cups.

The benevolent matriarch pushed aside strings of peppers, onions, and tobacco drying over the bed to make room for our mosquito nets. That gave us our cue to prepare for the night. When I pulled out a Scripture booklet to read by the dim light, the curious folk gathered to see it. One of the girls brought a burning stick and sat down beside me. "This book," I said, "has words from the God in Heaven. It's in my language, but we have one in Chinese. Would you like to see it?"

She nodded eagerly. The family crowded more closely as I pulled out a Chinese Gospel of John. Turning to John 3:16, I read, or rather recited, the very first Bible verse we had learned in Chinese. At first the group said they could not understand me, but when I repeated the verse again and again, they began to recite it after me.

They understand! I thought with elation.

"Can anyone here read Chinese?" Edith asked.

A shy lad acknowledged that he could as his grand-mother beamed. We gave him the book, and he promised to read it to the others.

"Do you pray to your God?" someone asked.

"Yes, we do," we replied.

"Show us how," our listeners urged.

Edith responded with the Lord's Prayer, which we'd also learned for our first language exam. She continued on and gave thanks for those who had welcomed us into their home. We longed for more language to respond to their questions.

For a time after we had zipped ourselves into our still-damp sleeping bags, folks sat chatting quietly around the fire, examining whatever we had left outside our nets. They tried on our shoes and coats and sampled water from our canteens. Then, one by one, as they finished their smokes, they left the room.

I lay thanking my heavenly Father for His care throughout the day and for shelter now in this home. Rain pattered on the roof. Baby ducklings peeped in a basket across the room. Cattle and hogs snored and breathed heavily just beyond a half-door partition. A couple of times in the night Granny came into the room to look around and to check on the fire.

The household stirred at dawn. The carriers did not appear until much later. Edith and I gratefully accepted the flat corn cakes and black tea brought to us. Our carriers, unaccustomed to such food, refused it. Without rice and opium, they grumbled and dallied.

Around nine o'clock, when the sun had spread

across the valley floor, we bade farewell to our open-hearted hosts. We had not gone far before the men insisted they could no longer carry us. Walking the rest of the trail, we reached the ridge called "Gospel Mountain" just before noon.

Missionary children and their little tribal friends ran to meet us as we picked our way down the last steep incline. "Why didn't you come last night?" they wanted to know.

"Ah, that's a long story! We'll tell you all about it later." Those stories made good nap-time tales for many days!

Rest, nourishing food, walks in the cool mountain air, and old-fashioned quinine, along with a new drug called Atabrine, finally conquered my chilling fevers.

From the window of my room above the Gospel Hall I watched nimble, barefoot men and women in patched, tattered clothing working the craggy slopes. I enjoyed their lively chatter and the laughter of their children. What I saw and heard made me long to get to know these people.

When I met my tribal neighbors, I found them buoyantly happy in spite of their straitened circumstances. Over one hundred gathered for their annual Bible conference, some from as far away as fifty miles. I watched them arriving, some descending from high mountain passes. Each brought a week's supply of food, mostly ground corn, in a basket on his or her back. Their singing delighted me. Bursts of harmony, when the sopranos and tenors lilted up to the highest notes, sent chills up and down my spine. I loved being awakened by their melodies.

As these folk listened to the messages given or translated into their language, I could sense their hunger for God's Word. The last day of conference began as usual with an hour of prayer. Then, while shadows still lingered in the valley, we walked the mile to a sparkling pool at the base of a cascading waterfall for the baptism of an elderly couple and eight younger people.

The final afternoon a pastor from a neighboring tribal group gave the challenge to a hushed audience. I sat among them, and at the close of the service received from their hands bread and wine, emblems of our Savior's death for us. That hour confirmed again the incredible oneness we have in Jesus Christ, regardless of race, culture or background. In those moments I thanked God from the depths of my heart for every circumstance, good and ill, that had brought me to that hour. I wondered if one day if I would share such oneness with Nosu people, with whom I was to work. I hoped so.

Actually I would have liked to stay right there and minister among these charming mountain people. But rapidly changing political events made my return to Luhsien imperative. ■

ᔕ10ભ
Return to the Valley

On my return to Luhsien I found the autumn short-term Bible school in progress. I ate my midday meal with the students and enjoyed getting to know them and learning from them idiomatic language and customs not found in our textbooks.

Once a week I joined some of the students and staff on a trip to a tiny chapel about five miles from the city. The three-sided, mud-walled structure stood in a grove of trees on the crest of a hill. A local Christian family had donated the land for it.

Each morning hundreds of farmer folk with baskets of fresh produce passed the little shelter on the way to city markets. We planned to arrive about noon, when folk began to return home. Many stopped to rest for awhile in the shade before continuing. Gourd dippers hung from a split-bamboo trough that brought cool water from a nearby spring. The farmers sat chatting on backless benches brought from the neighboring farmhouse or on carrying poles laid across their empty baskets. Some gathered around to read the fresh posters and gospel tracts we fastened to the earthen walls with sharp, wooden pegs. Those silent witnesses would remain after we had gone.

Some produce-sellers ambled over to the chapel to listen to the students give short messages and sing. Others listened from a distance. After taking a short rest and listening for ten minutes or so, folk were usually ready to move on. New arrivals took their places.

We recognized some who stopped week by week. Others, with heads averted, passed quickly by. Most gladly received the gospel literature we offered. A few bought our colorful Scripture posters to put on the plain walls of their homes. Late returnees, usually those with unsold goods, stopped for only a cold drink. They needed to hasten home before nightfall.

Around three in the afternoon, we gathered up the remaining literature while the men hoisted the benches onto their shoulders. We all made our way to the farmhouse by a narrow path between paddy fields. The hospitable family at the farmhouse kept an eye on our activities and had a hot, tasty meal prepared for us. Having not eaten since morning, we were hungry. Not even sleeping piglets near the doorway could ruin our appetites! Nor did we mind the dogs and baby chicks waiting at our feet for bones or dropped bits of food.

From where I sat I enjoyed the scene outside the

door. Ducks, chickens, geese, and water buffalo roamed freely about stacks of straw in the freshly swept farmyard. On high racks near the house, flat bamboo trays of peanuts and soy beans dried in the afternoon sun. In the not too distant future this peaceful scene would turn to devastating shambles.

After the meal we committed to God the scattered Seed we had sown and turned homeward.

My early months in China had put me in touch with city neighbors, tribal mountain people, students, and lowland farmers. Opportunity now awaited me among a new group of people.

A large military complex had moved from the east coast ahead of the rapidly encroaching communist army. They relocated a few miles downriver from us. A number of Christians among the employees transferred with the installation. We learned about the group when they sent a deputation asking for someone to come teach them. Philip, the young pastor, and our senior missionary, Fred, responded gladly to their request.

One day, when illness kept Fred home, I went in his place. Pastor Tzang, an older teacher at the short-term Bible school, would preach in the morning, and I was to teach Fred's afternoon English Bible class.

The friends from the government complex came to show us the way. For a couple of miles we traveled by rickshaws over mucky streets alive with morning shoppers. At the far end of the city our escorts located a boat to take us downriver. After haggling over the price, initially overpriced because of my white face, we climbed aboard.

The swift current took only twenty minutes to transport us to the small village where our friends had canvas carrying chairs waiting. At the gates of the huge military factory we gained admittance without question, in spite of tight security.

Over fifty adults listened attentively to the pastor's message. Warmly, though off-key, they sang the songs someone had written out on a classroom blackboard.

After that meeting we chatted until called to dinner. When our friends asked if I could use chopsticks, the pastor assured them that I could. Never at a loss for words, he kept the conversation lively as we ate. I squeezed in an occasional "yes" or "no."

At one-thirty, with pounding heart, I stepped into a well-filled room. I gave a short, well-practiced introduction in Chinese, then began my English Bible study. These highly qualified men and women understood English well, and I felt an immediate rapport with them.. The forty-five minutes of teaching and happy sharing from bilingual New Testaments passed quickly.

As soon as the class finished, we needed to head home. It was November, and the days were growing shorter. A trip against the current still lay ahead of us. Pastor Tzang climbed into his chair, and I stepped into mine. Unfortunately when the men lifted me, the canvas split! When I got out, inspection showed that three quarters of the seat had torn from the backrest. Those bidding us farewell called to halt the pastor,

already well beyond the gate. He returned as the
carriers made a hasty repair with ropes laced around
the frame. "Try again!" they invited. This time the
canvas ripped away completely!

We could do nothing but wait for another chair.
When we finally reached the river, I realized the
seriousness of our delay. "No boats going upriver
tonight," someone told us.

Our carriers would go no farther. "The path along
the river is too bad to travel in the darkness," they
explained.

Evil-minded bystanders flung slanderous insults at
my chaperone. "Where are you going with a foreign
woman this time of the evening?" they called. Pastor
Tzang studiously ignored their crude taunts.

Then someone spotted a boat a little distance upriver just pushing off. Calling to the boatmen, we
hurried down slick steps to the river and ran along the
water's edge to the craft. As there were no women on
the boat for me to sit with, the pastor asked three men
seated next to the side of the boat to scoot toward the
center so that I could sit on the outside. He did not sit
down himself until I had laid my Bible on the seat
between us. Pastor Tzang knew our more relaxed
Western ways, but would not compromise his own
culture.

We made slow progress upriver. Twice at swirling
rapids, we all got out. Other passengers scrambled to
the tow ropes. When I moved to help, the pastor
motioned me away. "You are a foreign teacher, a guest
in our country," he said. "It's not fitting for you to do

such tasks." Then he added, "Just as a woman is not to sit touching a man, neither is she to have her hand on the same rope with a man's hand."

I followed demurely behind. So that's why he had extended the handle of his umbrella instead of his hand when we descended those slippery steps! I wondered how many other *faux paus* I had made that day. I began to understand why the older man had come as my escort instead of the younger pastor and felt thankful to be learning Chinese customs from a true Christian gentleman.

Some days later I learned of another by-product of that eventful day. While waiting for lunch at the factory, I had chatted with Rachel, one of those who had shown us the way from the river. Several young-sters played around us. "Is anyone teaching these children about Jesus?" I had asked.

"No," she replied. "Won't you come teach them?"

"I'd like that," I said, "but my language is still inadequate. Maybe one day I can. Why don't you teach them?"

"I'm not qualified," she said. "Besides, I have no teaching materials."

Called at that moment to lunch, we could talk no more, but I felt burdened to pray. Five days later Rachel came to visit. Her first words thrilled me. "God has told me I am to teach the children. Will you help me prepare?" With Teacher Ho's help, the next Sun-day the children at the government factory heard about Jesus from one of their own.

I looked forward to returning to the factory to encourage Rachel with her class, but it was never to be. Within a few weeks the communists came. That installation was one of the first to fall into their hands. Many weeks passed before I saw Rachel again.

*D*espite uncertainties, the autumn Bible school continued to the end of term. As usual, it closed with the annual county-wide conference for all believers. Representatives flowed in from many district churches. Some lodged with relatives in the city. Most, wanting the extra hours of Christian fellowship with old friends, preferred to stay on the church compound.

The conference began on high notes of praise, rich and challenging. The speaker shared the burden God had given him of carrying the message of Jesus Christ all the way across central Asia to Jerusalem. "Messengers from the West brought the Gospel to us," he said. "Now our responsibility is to take the same Good News beyond China's borders to those who have never heard."

The first afternoon of the conference a telegram arrived, advising the keynote speaker to return to Chungking. After prayer, however, he chose to remain. With rumors and tensions rampant at the time, his quiet example of faith and prayerful confidence in God gave life-sustaining encouragement to others.

A meaningful communion service the final evening brought the conference to a triumphant close. Afterwards conference attendees gathered in little groups in the church or in other rooms, asking God to make them strong, wise, and faithful. Many talked and prayed into the early morning hours.

We rose well before daybreak to bid farewell to speakers, teachers, students and guests. As we bowed to pray with brothers and sisters in Christ on the steps of the church, at the bus stop or the river's edge, a hush invariably settled over those standing nearby. Several times I heard the words, "Look! The Christians are praying that God will keep them safe." We did pray for safety, but more for God to guard the hearts of our friends and keep them true to Himself through the days ahead. ■

‰11‰
"Liberation" and "Liberties"

After conference quiet enveloped the emptied mission compound. Two mornings later even the streets outside grew noiseless. City residents fled to the country; country people slipped into the city. The compound gateman kept the big front gates closed.

As the menacing stillness deepened, I embroidered the cover of a bag I was making for Teacher Ho's Christmas. The project gave my hands something to do, leaving my mind free to talk with the Lord.

At breakfast the next morning May came with a suggestion: "How would you like to learn how to make real English Christmas cake and pudding today?"

"Super!" I responded. It would help quieten the inevitable tension building in our hearts.

We spent the morning preparing the fruit and after

lunch blended the mixtures and set them to bake and steam. Mid-afternoon as I went to the kitchen to test the cake, a sputter of artillery in the distance broke the stillness. Peering out the windows, we saw soldiers running among the orange trees beyond the river. The conquest of Luhsien had begun.

A couple of days earlier we had decided to read a book at mealtime to keep our conversation off the encroaching warfare. That evening Fred had just taken up the book to read, when exploding shells rattled windows and shook the house. We cast questioning glances toward our reader. Fred's nod of assent sent us flying down the steps to street level. Ho-Ho, Anna, Philip, and Andrew had already gathered outside. We prayed together and waited, talking softly.

Twice the bombing quieted, then erupted again. When finally a tenuous silence settled over the city, we felt it reasonably safe to return to our house and went inside.

Our half-finished supper and the open book still cluttered the dining table. In the kitchen we found the well-steamed pudding in a dry pot on a cold stove. *Is this how things will look to those left behind when the Lord returns?* I wondered.

Though all remained quiet, we decided to bring bedding from the upstairs rooms and make up pallets on the office floor for the night. We lay down fully clothed to try to rest.

*P*erhaps two hours had elapsed when what
sounded like an old-fashioned Fourth of July
jolted us from sleep. "Your emancipators have come!"
we heard town criers shout, jarring our foggy heads.
"Open your gates! Come! Welcome them!"

Scrambling from my makeshift bed, I followed others to the front of the compound. Gatey stood trembling in the darkness, his hand on the great latch of
the big wooden doors. "Don't open them yet!" called
Fred. "Stand by; we'll go upstairs to see what is going
on."

Climbing the narrow steps in the gatehouse to

rooms recently vacated by conference guests, we cautiously unlocked the shutters and peered out. The criers, carrying flaming torches, dashed in and out of dark lanes and alleys with their message. A babbling mob spewed into the street below. I looked at my watch. It was just past midnight, December 4, 1949.

Abruptly the babble of voices organized into a synchronized chant of welcome to the conquerors. Then we saw them! Down the street seven youthful soldiers marched in single file, twelve paces apart, carbines swinging easily at their sides. Except for the leader, each soldier wore a nationalist army uniform with jacket and cap turned inside out. Each crumpled cap sported a newly attached red star. I shivered.

The tumult and hubbub faded as the parade moved on toward center city. We closed the windows and retraced our steps. "We will leave the gates closed," Fred told Gatey, "at least until daylight."

We mounted the broad steps past the church. "Come in and sit a while," called Teacher Ho over her shoulder.

Ho-Ho poured each of us a cup of hot water from a thermos on the table in her home. We nibbled watermelon seeds and warmed our hands on the cups. A tiny flame hissed from the wick in the shallow bowl of oil at the center of the table. It cast flickering shadows across tired faces. We bowed to give thanks for safety—then the room grew silent. Each of us wondered how our new "liberties" would develop. Deep in our hearts we held to the confidence that God, who knew the future, would remain true to His promise: "I will never leave thee nor forsake thee." I asked Him to keep me true to mine.

After that night of "liberation," life on the streets returned to a surface normal. Only a few adults came to the worship service that Sunday morning. Not a child turned up for Sunday school. The next day schools plunged into feverish preparations for newly declared government holidays.

Though heavy rains delayed the celebrations, two days before Christmas we watched school children, in bright new uniforms, goose-stepping proudly behind marching bands. They shouted the slogans printed on huge red banners they carried aloft. Pictures of Marx, Lenin, and Stalin dominated the parade.

Our Christmas Day service, though more subdued than usual, renewed in us the joy of Jesus' birthday. A few came from country churches and from the soap factory. None came from the downriver plant.

Sunny and clear, the day after Christmas seemed ideal for an outing. We packed a picnic lunch and walked to a famous high cliff. Centuries earlier, someone had carved the account of a famous battle in beautiful, flowing Chinese characters on the cliff face. A river flowed swiftly nearby. The beauty, fresh air, and fellowship provided the break we all needed. On our return to the city we nodded cordially to surprised soldiers we met along the way.

Two days later we received visitors from the Foreign Affairs Bureau. "We've come to see how things are for you now," they said. "Is there anything we can do to help you? We want you to feel secure and free from anxiety," they assured us. Concluding their visit, they added uneasily, "Oh, by the way, we think it best for you not to ramble out into the hills. There could still be enemy soldiers out there, you know."

We got the message.

*E*arly in the new year we became increasingly aware of an incessant, pulsating rhythm of music or drumbeat. It continued both day and night and had a strange numbing effect.

About the same time communist cadres assigned all able-bodied adults to three different groups. Ten family members made up the first group, fifty near neighbors the second, and one hundred people from a local district formed the third group. These groups would facilitate indoctrinating the populace with the new communist ideologies. Attendance and participation in each group was obligatory. Group leaders considered exceptions only after a supplicant had submitted a written request.

Christians found that their group parleys often conflicted with regular church functions. Church meeting hours were changed to relieve the conflict, only to have the time for group sessions again changed to conflict. The modifications did not seem coincidental.

People grew uncertain and uneasy.

To encourage friends, we continued to visit them in their homes. We also continued going to the soap factory for the weekly children's Bible story hour—

until our friends living there suggested we stop coming as long as soldiers billeted there remained. The soldiers did not leave.

Worship services, prayer meetings, Bible classes, and baptismal class (all now with uncertain hours) continued into the first quarter of the year. The vacation Bible school at Chinese New Year, the last of February, drew a good number of children.

About five months into the new regime visits from the Bureau of Foreign Affairs increased. The tenor of the Bureau's communications grew firmer, and each visit brought added restrictions. With threats thinly veiled, officials told us, "Our only concern is for your welfare and safety." One day, citing unrest in the countryside as their reason, they advised us not to leave the city. We were not surprised. News of landlords executed as part of land reform gave us an idea of the real reason for keeping us in the city, where we could not witness the executions.

We yearned to go again to encourage friends in the country churches who had been to conference or short-term Bible schools. I especially missed our visits to the little wayside chapel on market days.

The day after one of our regular open-air meetings in town, officials came again. "We still fear for your safety," they said awkwardly. "Hoodlums roam the streets these days. It's all right for you to hold meetings here on your property," they continued, "but it is best that you do not hold them elsewhere."

Weeknight meetings in a small gate-house room

continued to draw those too shy to go up to the main church. A deputation from the police came again. This time the senior officer wore full uniform. "We observe ruffians, known by us, coming into your little chapel. You are therefore no longer to hold meetings there. You may hold them in your church, but not in the room that opens onto the street." Six months after occupation the last door for widespread evangelism had closed.

Our opportunities to reach out to needy neighbors also withered under increasing restrictions. An aged blind woman we used to visit often begged her daughter-in-law to have us come again. Teacher Ho and I promised to go.

Before we entered the home the daughter-in-law glanced anxiously toward the house of the local cadre who kept a watchful eye on neighborhood activities. Once safely inside, we climbed the familiar steps to where Granny lived alone in a far corner of the loft above the kitchen. To keep her from moving about, someone had removed all the floorboards except those in her tiny area. Teacher Ho, who had brought along some fresh eggs for her, took an egg from her basket and laid it in the gnarled hand stretched out to receive it. Lifting the treasure to her nose, the old woman smiled a sweet, toothless thanks.

After Teacher Ho read Scripture and prayed with her we picked our way carefully back across the open beams to the steps and descended. We were never able to return.

As 1950 developed, officials came day after day to inquire into every facet of our personal lives. Their rapid-fire questions had to be answered in detail and on the spot. Our examiners wanted to know the history of our grandparents, parents, brothers and sisters.

"In what year did your grandparents buy land in America? How many acres did they buy? What did they pay for it? Were they very rich? Name all the places your parents ever lived. To which political party does your family belong? To what party do you belong? Have you a communist party in America? Why don't you belong to it? Where did you go to school? Give the dates and length of time at each school. Is your father a landowner? If so, why did you work to pay for your college? What kind of work have you done? What was your wage at each job? List the occupation of each family member. Have you ever been to Russia? Why not? Why did you come to China?" And so forth and so forth and so forth!

Because of harassment each time we left the compound, we stopped going out unless absolutely necessary. With less opportunity for ministry, I turned more and more to language learning—in particular to the new "in" vocabulary even our non-official visitors began using.

We released our water carrier/gardener because of limited activities, growing financial limitations, and more time to do the work ourselves. He begged to continue with us, but we could not keep him. Brother One, our long-time cook, remained. In fact, our official visitors counseled us to keep him on, saying, "As teachers in our country, you should have such help in your home."

Later we learned Brother One had been assigned to keep an eye on all our activities and report them regularly to the Foreign Affairs Bureau. Our loyal helper now trod a difficult path.

T he relentless indoctrination meetings began having their intended effect. Fear, like thick clouds, settled over hearts. Planted suspicion fanned flames of hate into white heat. Fewer and fewer people came to church meetings, fearful of the scrutiny of those sent to "observe" at such gatherings.

As church attendance dwindled, we decided to hold services in one of the smaller Sunday school rooms. Shortly after that, representatives from the Promotion Department came to visit the pastor. "Is it true that you no longer use your large church hall? What a great pity for such a building to sit unused!" they said. "It would be a very suitable place for the exhibition we are planning. May we borrow the building for a week?"

Request granted! We had no choice.

Workmen came and whitewashed away the large Chinese characters at the front of the chapel. "Jesus Christ, the Light of the World" was replaced with, "World Communism, Our Hope." Communist mottoes appeared as well on side walls that once proclaimed God's Word.

When the exhibit opened, huge crowds came.

Teachers herded their students through the displays, and group leaders came with the adults under their tutelage. Pastor Philip and Andrew, who lived in rooms beside the church, chatted with many visitors and gave gospel literature and Scripture portions to any who wanted them.

On the third day police took the two young men to the station for questioning. "Why," the authorities wanted to know, "are you giving out anti-communist literature without permission at a public exhibit?"

"This is our habit when visitors come to our home," Pastor Philip and Andrew responded honestly.

The two were jailed.

Teacher Ho, called to the police station, learned that she might speak briefly to the prisoners when she brought their daily food.

In the mission house we prayed unceasingly for our colleagues. Teacher Ho cautioned us to remain indoors. After each trip to the jail with food, she came to brief us on the latest developments and to pray.

"If all literature given out is collected and brought to us, you may be released," authorities told the jailed men four days later.

When the two told Teacher Ho, she and Anna immediately set out to visit the homes of friends, asking for any literature they could find. "It doesn't matter when you got it," they told folk. The two women collected over a hundred pieces of the offending literature and took it to the police station. That evening Philip and Andrew were released.

*T*he very next morning, however, officers came to see the parolees. "You now have a prison record," they said. "Therefore we must have the complete text of every message you plan to give. It is to be written out and submitted for examination three days before it is given."

Complying with that order proved no small task. Yet the men rejoiced that at least one person would read the text of each message submitted. He would also read the accompanying Scripture telling of God's way of salvation.

The exhibition in the church continued four weeks. Shortly after it closed another request came for the building's use. "We urgently need more facilities for government workers," the official from the Housing Commission said. "An unused building like this could easily be made into very suitable apartments."

Even before workers completed the remodeling, on-the-spot surveillance personnel moved in. They dismissed Gatey, our faithful gate-keeper, telling him to return with his family to the country. Now no one entered or left the compound unobserved or unquestioned. Tensions built, both without and within.

*C*ash-transfer problems at the post office also stretched our faith. "Well, folks," Fred announced one day at lunch, "Still no money at the post office." He had gone five days running, expecting money from CIM in Shanghai. "Not only that," he went on, "the cook just told me this is the last of our rice. We have no cash to buy more."

"Liberation" and "Liberties"

As we bowed our heads to pray about this urgent need, we heard a strange sound at the front door. Fred went to the door, but seeing no one, came back to the table. We continued to pray. The soft tapping came again. "Some prankster out there," Fred con-

cluded as he pushed his chair from the table. This time we followed. Cautiously he parted the curtain, then opened the door a crack. Stepping back, he flung open the door and exclaimed, laughing, "Aha! So *you're* the culprit!"

Tied by a string to the doorknob, a fish flapped its tail against the door. We joined the laughter, then looked out to see who might have brought it. We saw only a black-slippered heel disappear around a corner. It surely looked like Ho-Ho's heel, but our dear friend never acknowledged that she was God's raven. We gave thanks to our heavenly Provider, both for the gift and the one who delivered it.

The next day on his return from the post office, Fred burst into the house calling, "Our money has come!" We laughed and cried together, thanking God for His timely mercies and faithful supply.

Our heavenly Father was teaching us to trust Him more fully—a lesson we would all need in days so near at hand. ■

๑ 12 ๏

Crucible of Fear

*L*uhsien's unusually wet and cold summer of 1950, combined with the increasing tensions, triggered acute arthritis for May. As resolutely as she tried to carry on, the onset of severely inflamed and painful joints made it necessary for her to seek medical help not locally available.

When Fred sought to obtain the required travel permit to take her to Chungking, he received a firm "No! The only permits being granted to foreigners these days are to leave the country."

When Fred returned with the bad news, cold fear gripped my heart. To the Lord I cried: "*O, Father, how can Dorothy and I stay here alone? Fred and May have been in China for many years. They know the language and culture well. Dorothy and I are new and barely articulate. Besides,* I ended lamely, *You know we don't get on too well together. You won't make us stay here alone, will You?*" I did not get my answer right away.

When mission leaders granted Fred and May leave to return to England, they arranged for another senior couple to replace them. But authorities also refused to grant travel permits to the replacement couple.

Though May's painful disability continued, I found it hard to pray for a quick granting of their exit permits. Giving thanks in the circumstances also seemed beyond me. Instead, I begged that Dorothy and I might be granted leave to go with them.

Looking back now, I can see how the Lord used the circumstances to test my promise. But my "thanksgiving key" lay largely unused at the time I most needed it. My peace departed and fears spiralled.

*I*n those days the consistent example of Anna, the elderly vegetable seller who lived near Teacher Ho, shamed me. In circumstances far more troubling than mine, she maintained a quiet peace and always found something to be thankful for. As a young bride, she had come with her husband from the far southeast of China. Not long after they came west her husband died. Too poor to return home, she stayed on alone. Though I understood very little of her distinctively south China dialect, I learned one of her oft-used phrases: *"Gom-she, Ju!"*—"Thank you, Jesus!"

Before dawn every day except Sunday, Anna went to the riverside to buy vegetables from farmers bringing produce to market. These she hawked up and down narrow alleys to regular customers. She usually returned home by noon with a few wilted vegetables for herself. As living conditions grew more difficult for all, not infrequently under those limp leaves she hid a little fruit, a small fish, or a bit of meat which she had traded for some of her vegetables. She brought these as gifts to one and another of us on the compound. With a deep bow and a broad smile, she would say, "For God's servants."

Oh, that I had learned to be as accepting and thankful!

As summer turned to autumn, we heard, almost daily, shots and shouts from the parade grounds just ouside the city's west gate. Those sounds were not shots to start a contest, nor cheers at a game.

Every time I heard those ominous sounds, my mind replayed a scene I had happened on one day when returning from the post office. Two men carried a third man, all three headed for execution. I should have thanked God that I was not required to be a part of the cheering crowd at those executions. Fear stifled thanksgiving.

In mid-November the day I dreaded came—the day Fred and May held in their hands their exit permits.

Before they could make travel arrangements, however, Fred and May needed to have a local person as their guarantor. He would take responsibility to pay any debts discovered after they left. The guarantor would also be responsible for any words Fred and May might say that were unfavorable to the current regime. In spite of inflammatory propaganda, a loyal church elder trusted his missionary friends and agreed to stand. We thanked God for such courage, knowing that fabricated accusations could cost him dearly.

Endless other matters made visits to various government offices necessary. These included notarizing the signature of the person now authorized to sign postal money orders and receive money from the bank. Officials needed to know the name of the new person now serving as head of household and representative for mission affairs. A "notice of departure" had to be published for three consecutive days in the local newspaper—to allow time for grievances to be reported to the police before the people concerned left. Until our colleagues completed all these matters, they could not book river passage.

Fred and May did all they could to cushion Dorothy and me from problems after their departure. Fred arranged with a government construction company to receive the main house and back garden at the end of the year. The semi-detached office building at a lower level, where Dorothy and I would live, remained in our possession—as did the old storage building opposite the offices. A small, grassy lawn separated the two. We hoped this area, at the center of the complex and not far from Teacher Ho's quarters, would provide us with a fair degree of privacy and safety.

Before Fred and May had completed all necessary arrangements to leave, a telegram came from Dr. Jim Broomhall asking me to come immediately to Nosuland to help in the medical work there. Though I had been designated to join that ministry and wanted to go, such a move was now impossible.

The next day an even more jolting telegram came from our mission headquarters in Shanghai. It advised the evacuation of all missionary personnel. Concluding that God had answered my prayers, I cried for sheer joy. Now we could all go together! I was wrong.

Fred inquired if he and May might delay their departure until exit permits could be granted for Dorothy and me. The answer was brusque: "You have asked to leave the country. If you do not go now, an indefinite cancellation of your travel passes could result."

Fred and May could not risk such a proviso. They would have to leave without us. Eight days before Christmas they did. Dorothy and others from the compound went to the wharf to see them off. Not trusting myself with such a parting, I said goodbye to them in the home. After seeing them off in rickshaws at the front gate, I fled back into the vacant house.

Only work, I felt, would keep me rational. There was plenty of that! Just fourteen days remained before we had to have everything cleared out of the sixty-year-old mission house and evacuate the place.

For the moment I let myself wander back into the dining room, where, as a family, we had often shared, prayed together, and claimed promises from God's Word. Standing beside the table and thinking, *We won"t need such a large table now,* I started to remove a board. Instead, I crumpled onto it. "I can't— I can't go on," I sobbed into the emptiness.

But the room was not empty. God was there. ■

℘13℞

Surprises in the Attic

An hour or so after Dorothy and the others had gone to see our seniors to the boat, I heard them return. I fled to the attic with my red, swollen eyes and began to work there. "We're back," Dorothy called from the foot of the stairs. "I'm going to the office to work on accounts."

Dorothy had her own quiet way of working off anguish. Mine was plowing into the hoard of things left behind by generations of former residents.

With resounding clatter I tossed discards from the outside attic door to the ground two floors below. Brother One, hearing the racket, came to see what was going on, then lent assistance. We moved into the mass of accumulated cast-offs. Here was a pair of crutches, there an old-fashioned dress form, beside them rusty metal frames once used to stretch and dry heavy woolen stockings. At the far side of the attic a wicker baby basket and a couple of battered trunks stood beside a bent bicycle wheel. If those things could have spoken, they would have told endless stories of those who had lived and worked from this old home over the years.

As we made our way forward, I came upon a machete on the floor. "Whatever is this?" I exclaimed.

"Oh, that! It's a jungle knife we use to cut down banana trees and hack out brambles in the back garden," answered the cook.

Taking the long knife to the doorway for a closer look, I saw, with horror, an insignia identifying it as a military weapon. "We will have to take this to the police," I told Brother One, remembering an early mandate of the new government that all weapons be turned in.

"Oh, no—you can't do that!" he countered. "It must be destroyed."

My confidence in our long-time cook rose a notch. I carried the offending weapon to my bedroom and buried it in a drawer.

Our mission leaders had directed us to leave the property clean and in good order. Nothing must remain that could incriminate us. That included personal photos, letters, books, and maps, even maps in old Bibles.

"Whatever can we do with all these things?" I groaned.

"Well," the cook suggested, "the broken bed frames, stools, high chairs, and other wooden things can be split into kindling. Those pieces of broken window panes and mirrors can be sold. The cracked water jars, leaky kettles and old lids will probably sell too."

Appreciation for my loyal helper went up another step!

In a far corner among other cast-offs we found a dial-less radio with dangling, corroding wires. The cook eyed it with interest. "Umm, I might be able to sell some of that for spare parts."

"But you will take care, won't you?" I warned.

Brother One nodded solemnly. I breathed a sigh of relief that we had not known about the old radio before. We had been asked repeatedly about equipment that could receive or transmit messages to the United States. Though our interrogators never seemed to believe us, we had told them in all honesty, "No, we have none."

Now a warning flashed in my brain. *Don't forget, Brother One is expected to report everything done in this house to the Foreign Affairs Bureau. He could make a nasty situation out of this.*

We kept doggedly at our task. Darkness had nearly closed in when I came upon a shoe-box-sized carton with a Red Cross label. Something heavy rolled inside as I picked it up. Opening it, I wondered aloud what the oval-shaped hunk of scored metal could be.

"Oh, that's a Japanese hand grenade," Brother One replied casually. Seeing the shock on my face, he added, "Don't worry. The pin is out! Soldiers brought it to show the pastor a long time ago, after the war."

Chills tingled up and down my spine as I thought how tomorrow's newspaper headlines might read: "*U.S. missionary secreting deadly weapons and sending clandestine messages to Washington*"!

I took the second offender to my bedroom. *What else*, I wondered, *will we uncover?* That night I went to bed emotionally and physically drained.

*E*arly the next morning the cook went to market as usual. I wrestled in prayer. Would he report the banned discoveries? When he returned alone, he came to find me. "We must dispose of that jungle knife and grenade today," he said.

Later that evening, while others gathered for the prayer service, I slipped into a warm coat and brought the machete and hand grenade from my room. The cook went for the hoe, saying, "We will bury the grenade first." But where?

We decided on a sheltered corner in the back garden. I fingered the cold, iron ball in my pocket while the cook dug a hole. Kneeling, I laid the grenade in the pit. Brother One raked the freshly disturbed earth back and covered it with leafy debris.

Back in the kitchen, we decided the machete must be cut into pieces.

Doing it was another matter! With every thrust of the hacksaw, the hard, tortured steel screeched its protest into the still night air. Each time we hesitated, afraid of listening ears or watchful eyes. Finally the long monster lay in four pieces. We took three of them to the garden and drove them deep into the ground beside gnarled old tree roots. The remaining piece we put in the stove to burn off its fiber handle. Later, when our efforts to file away the incriminating "U.S. Army" insignia simply made it brighter, we buried it under a flagstone in the kitchen floor.

After cleaning up the filings and putting away the saw and file, we paused to thank God for closing the ears of those who might have questioned our activities. We asked that our infractions would never cause trouble to anyone again.

One concern remained. The cook had once mentioned having seen a gun being offered to a former missionary. As mission policy forbade the possession of firearms, I doubted he had received the gift. But we needed to be certain. In the next few days we searched everywhere, finally concluding that the gun had either been refused or disposed of. It would not be so easy to dispose of Brother One's words should he decide to talk.

We continued to clear out the old house. At Ho-Ho's suggestion, we offered bedding, clothing, and household equipment for sale at give-away prices.

After three days the police came to investigate. "Have you a merchant's license?" they challenged. "If not, what you are doing is illegal and must be stopped immediately."

Gathering up the remaining things, we wondered what to do now. We could not give stuff away. To do so would be seen as bribery. Recipients would be

punished for accepting the gifts. Nor could we leave
personal things behind.

Two large clay stoves, normally used to boil laundry on wash days, solved our dilemma. We stoked the
flames day after day with items our friends could have
used and books we would have liked to take with us.
As we fanned the fires to lessen smoke, we prayed no
one would come to investigate and that no stray spark
would ignite a fire outside.

Only the sure knowledge that God watched over
us kept me on course those days. Very little
"Christmas spirit" found its way into our feverish
activities that December. Yet deep in our hearts,
Dorothy and I knew that Jesus Christ, that Babe of
Bethlehem, had come, even for those who were turning our world upside down.

We took to the three small office rooms we would
occupy only what we needed for a temporary stay.
The last day of December we swept and thoroughly
cleaned the main house for the last time. It had never
been so spotless.

In the afternoon inspectors from the construction
company came and looked through the building. They
nodded approvingly as we handed them the keys.
"We have two requests," we said. "Will you ask your
personnel, please, to use the rear gate? And may we
continue to harvest vegetables from the garden and
bury our garbage there?"

The officials agreed to both requests. "We will move
in tomorrow," they said, and departed.

That evening, New Year's Eve, yelps of glee and bursts of laughter from the old home startled us. *Whatever can that be?* we wondered as we went to our door.

Ogling eyes met ours at every window in the house above us. Newly inducted military cadets had taken possession. We stepped back into our room, secured the doors, and hung sheets to cover the tall windows. That night we rested uneasily.

Next morning, with a loud crash, locks on doors that secured our section of the compound fractured. Rampaging youth poured down the steps to our quarters. With a stick, they poked a hole through one of the windows and pushed aside the covering. Calling vulgar names, they peered into our room.

A sudden sharp command from above halted the assault. The mob retreated.

For ten days we heard the youthful soldiers' horseplay and the frequent breaking of glass and splintering of wood. Then the occupants left as suddenly as they had come.

The day the soldiers left, Brother One went to bury garbage and returned to tell of shocking devastation. He spoke, too, of incensed government workers who had come to survey the damage. They had seen the property as we had left it. Now they gazed angrily at the begrimed shambles.

I never went up to view the destruction. Female political prisoners were brought in to clean the filth-smeared walls, windows, and floors and to clear away the dirty straw on which the soldiers had slept.

When the prisoners finished cleaning, government construction personnel moved in. Happily those occupants were amiable, and they neither embarrassed nor harassed us. Some of the women secretaries, in fact, came to ask for help with English and expressed shame over the regrettable affair.

*B*y mid-January Dorothy and I began to de-celerate and plan for a belated Christmas.

With a fling of rare extravagance, our faithful cook brought wood from the trash pile in the back garden and laid a fire in the long-unused office fireplace. He then went to the kitchen to prepare a Christmas dinner. He outdid himself with produce from the garden and two tins of food we had hoarded.

For a few tranquil hours Dorothy and I sat before the cozy, crackling fire, eating, dreaming, and talking about our Australian and American families. Ruminating on the weeks we had faced with such trepidation and fear, we recognized how wonderfully God had neutralized danger, given wisdom, help, strength, and health throughout the big move—and how much we had to be thankful for.

That evening Teacher Ho accepted our invitation to come and share some of our late-Christmas goodies. Talk turned easily to worship and praise as we considered the wonders of our Savior's matchless love.

What a special day! ■

⁊14⅋

Commitment
Under Fire

By the end of the first year of communist occupation in our part of China the new government
had instituted radical changes. The new rules
touched daily life for everyone.

Church attendance dwindled. Church offerings
shrank and along with them the income for the work
Teacher Ho carried on among women and children. I
was not overly surprised, therefore, when one afternoon she announced, "Today I went to a factory that
manufactures small spinning machines. I think I could
learn to spin." Without a hint of bitterness, she continued, "The cadres encourage home industries, and I
believe I can support myself this way."

I was the one who smarted as I thought of all
Ho-Ho had done for so many people over the years. I
resented those who no longer considered her ministry
worthwhile.

Ho-Ho went to classes at the factory to learn the technique of spinning. A couple of weeks later workmen installed the new equipment in her guest room. I watched as she proudly surveyed her new machine. She sat down to demonstrate. Though intended to spin fourteen strands at a time, her efforts produced but two knobby threads. "With practice, I will do it right," dear Ho-Ho said confidently.

I went down often to watch the new spinner's progress. On one occasion I found her standing despondently beside the unresponsive apparatus. "You try," she said.

Convinced that two deft hands and strong feet could make it operate effectively, I sat down. My efforts, however, were equally hopeless.

Ho-Ho sent the machine back to the factory for readjustment. When it came back six weeks later, it still produced only half the normal output. Ho-Ho had a dud. She did not have finances to purchase another or send this one for repair again. and we felt powerless to help her.

To increase production, I sometimes relieved Ho-Ho while she rested. Authorities expected her to return a full quota of thread week by week in exchange for the raw cotton her group leader brought her. Anna, too, came to help out after selling her vegetables. But we all knew that, at best, Ho-Ho would receive minimal income from her efforts.

A couple of months after our move from the main mission house authorities approached us for more housing. "We are short of accommodations for our government workers," said the spokesman. "Since you are leaving soon, we want to borrow these three rooms. You may live there," he said, indicating the old storage building across the tiny yard. Brother One already lived in one room at the end of the earthen-floored structure because his little cottage had also been transferred to the construction company.

Without questioning, we packed up and moved. A narrow kitchen/storage room separated our room from Brother One's. Dorothy and I divided our single room with a tall wardrobe. A table and two chairs fit snugly on one side of the bulky divider. With a tight squeeze, we could just get around our double bed on the other side. Trunks with our personal things provided "counter space" in the tiny kitchen. We shared Teacher Ho's washroom and toilet below.

Cramped living increased vexations. At one time of particular stress, I cried, "If I ever get out of here, I'll never be a missionary again!" Mercifully, the Lord did not hold me to that bitter outburst!

One balmy spring day we persuaded Brother One to help us dig up the yard at the front of our rooms so that we could make a small vegetable garden. Our new neighbors looked on with stoic interest. They had obviously not seen foreigners doing manual labor before.

Excitedly I watched as seedlings appeared. The plants leafed out, blossomed, and finally set tiny beans. One day at play the neighbors' children broke several of the bushes. The cook staked them up, and I gathered some of the young beans, doubtful they would develop on the damaged plants. Next day other bushes were toppled. I gathered more tender beans.

That evening three young women in uniform stood at our door. "We are from the Agricultural Department," they said, introducing themselves. "We've come to investigate a report that you are harvesting beans before they have matured . . . a waste of China's natural resources. Is that true?" they asked.

I acknowledged my misjudgment, received their caution, and thanked them for their trouble. But I wasn't *really* thankful! Inside I was fuming, especially when I saw the mother of the children step back from the window with a smug smile.

When our callers left, my first impulse was to go out and rip up the whole garden. But that, I knew, would ignite more trouble *and* could delay our exit. How I needed God's checks and controls those days!

Real panic broke out another day when the cook came back from burying garbage in the old garden. With trembling lips he stammered, "They're digging a night-soil pit right where we buried that hand grenade!"

The two of us stepped into the kitchen, asking for God's protection. When Brother One regained control, he retraced his steps to the garden on the pretext of gathering turnips. We already had a sufficient supply, but from the garden he could watch the digging from a distance. I waited below for his return.

An hour later, though it seemed much longer, Brother One returned with an armful of well-polished turnips. A smile lit his face. "Know what?" he said.

"No, what?" I asked.

"They dug the hole right up to within inches of the grenade. They are now preparing to cement the pit and seal all around the edges. That thing will be safe for years." He chuckled.

Day by day I was learning more of God's marvelous care for us.

A few weeks later I again grappled for control. Workmen, who claimed they came from a munitions plant, appeared at our door. "We're looking for saltpeter, used in the making of gunpowder," they said. "It is found in especially dirty places. We want to check here."

Thanks! I thought.

I was totally unprepared for what happened next. The spokesman plunged a small, drilling instrument into the dirt floor at my feet. Drawing it up, he touched his tongue to the tip of it. He nodded thoughtfully. Turning to the men waiting with picks and shovels behind him, he said, "Put the furniture outside."

Helplessly Dorothy and I looked on while the intruders emptied our room. "This won't take long. When we've finished here, we'll do up there." The man pointed with his chin toward the big house.

Brother One's words about a gun roared into my mind. Could the missionary offered the weapon have received it? Could he have disposed of it under the big house?

The workmen dug the hard-packed earth of our floor to the depth of nearly a foot. They completed the job by bringing a few baskets of wet, yellow clay to sprinkle on the uneven earth, creating a stippled effect. The men set the furniture inside and departed.

While keeping an eye on the excavators, Brother One had busied himself in the kitchen. He now came into our room to help arrange and level our furniture.

Teacher Ho also came up to see what had happened. When I told her what the foreman said about returning tomorrow to dig under the big house and shared my fears of what they might find there, she frowned. She stayed only long enough for us to pray together. Early the next morning, before the workmen arrived, she came in, announcing, "I'm spending the day with you. I will come every day until that job is done." I hugged her!

The old mission home stood on huge natural rocks, raising the building a couple of feet off the ground. Now, for five tormenting days, Ho-Ho, Dorothy and I knitted or sewed while workmen dragged basketful after basketful of earth from under it. As time passed, we realized that the excavators were not looking for saltpeter, but for anything hidden there. I cried with relief and thanksgiving when they stopped work at the kitchen floor not far from that identifying piece of the machete.

A few days after the excavations ended, our neighbors moved out. With deliberate care, they "accidentally" trampled the rest of our garden. When they had gone, the officer who told us to move from our rooms came to say that we might reclaim them if we wished.

"If we wished"?! The prospect of more space and separate rooms again made cleaning out the trash left behind positively pleasant. Our move had obviously been ordered to enable a thorough search of the grounds before we left the country.

Through those days of continuing government reforms, God used sharing times with our Chinese co-workers to encourage and strengthen us all. As testing fires intensified, His Spirit brightened promises, sharpened reproofs, and gave new insights into His Word.

One evening in April Teacher Ho came on a special errand. She often came just to chat, pray, or play a game of Chinese checkers. This time she seemed uneasy. Finally she revealed her mission. Speaking quietly, she said, "Pastor Philip, Andrew, the elders, and I have been talking. I must ask that you two no longer come to the church meetings. There's so much anti-foreign propaganda, and the people have been cautioned to stay away from any meeting if you are present." Her black eyes glistened with tears.

After that only Ho-Ho and a blind teen-ager braved reproach to visit us. We cherished their selfless love.

In the difficult weeks that followed an especially

precious moment stands out. Late one Sunday morning Teacher Ho came to our door. In her good hand she carried a small plate covered with a white handkerchief. Stepping into the room where Dorothy and I sat having our own worship time, she set the dish on the table. Sitting down, she lifted the cover. "This is for you," she whispered huskily. On the tiny dish we saw bread and wine, brought from the communion table below. "Philip asked me to bring this to you," she said, pausing to check her emotions. "He asked me to tell you that though you may no longer meet with us, we are still one in Christ."

Three pairs of eyes welled with tears as we remembered the One who had bound us together in Himself.
■

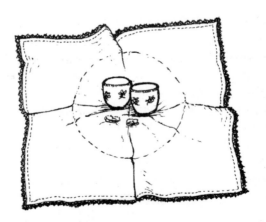

೫15ಌ
Meticulous Timing

*I*n spite of the trouble and turmoil of those days, the pink and white roses beside the house bloomed gloriously, and the citrus tree outside our door poured rich fragrance into the spring air. These should have encouraged me. Instead, I let my consuming desire to leave China so dominate my thinking that I became ill.

Dorothy brought some of the fragrant blossoms to my bedside; Teacher Ho brought the doctor. At the time I would have said I trusted God for His work in my life. In reality I wanted my will, not His.

Early in May the Health Department asked me to assist in a city-wide inoculation campaign. I appreciated the opportunity and enjoyed participating—until I became ill a second time. Dispirited, I spilled out a flood of bitter *Why?s.*

After I had spent three days of misery, God rebuked my sin of continual complaining. *Try giving thanks for these circumstances instead!* came His prompting.

Though I wondered how honest my prayer of thanksgiving could be, I tried to concentrate on the many things God had done for me. "I am Your child, Lord, because You gave Your Son Jesus as my Savior; I am thankful for Him," I told Him. "Thank You for being with me even now. Thanks for Dorothy, for dear Ho-Ho, the doctor and medicines. Thank You for bringing Rachel and her darling baby last week, for that little lull while the syringes and needles boiled so that Rachel and I could talk. Thank You for the love and trust she has in You, even though her husband is in labor camp. Thank You for keeping him in that hard place...." The list grew.

Finally I added, with some hesitation, "Lord, I am willing to stay here as long as You want me to stay."

The next morning I woke to find my fever had dropped, nausea and vomiting had ceased, and I was at peace. Thanking *had* worked!

*F*ive days later, when Dorothy and I returned from a busy afternoon of giving injections, the gate-keeper met us with a message: "This afternoon a policeman from the Provincial Headquarters came. You must go to see him this evening."

Seeing the apprehension on our faces, the gateman continued, "It's all right. Don't be afraid. I think your passes have come, but don't tell the police I told you!"

We raced to our rooms to tidy ourselves up a bit and to grab a bite to eat and then headed for the police station. We had just passed through our front gate when the gateman called to us, "Here he comes!"

The messenger approached us. "Your travel permits have come," he said. "You may leave as soon as there is a boat."

Hardly daring to believe our ears, we asked the policeman go with us to Teacher Ho's room and repeat his message to her. "It is true," he told her. "Their exit permits have been granted. All they will need to do is to put a three-day announcement in the paper."

"And what about guarantors?" Ho-Ho asked.

"That will not be necessary for them," he replied.

We thanked him, watched him turn away, and then, with tears, turned to Teacher Ho. "I saw the policeman this afternoon," she told us. "But he did not reveal his mission to me."

Dear *Saint* Ho-Ho exulted with us as we praised and prayed together.

Months later, in America, I learned that my home church in Indianapolis had had an all-night prayer meeting to ask God for my release from China. As far as we could calculate, that night of prayer coincided with the day I submitted to God's will and honestly applied my thanksgiving key in West China. God not only answers prayer, He refines with meticulous care.

Things on hold for months were now set in motion. But we had barely begun our final sorting and packing when ten police cadets came to our door. One of the young men stepped forward and smiled politely. "We've come to visit," he said.

We welcomed them and brought drinking water. "We hear you're going to leave China," they said, making casual conversation.

We nodded. I wondered if they hoped for a final English lesson.

"Why are you leaving?" they continued. "Don't you love China?"

We searched for acceptable, honest answers. Small talk finally gave way to awkward silences. Then one young man asked, "Are you all packed up?"

"No, we were just preparing to do that now," we said, hoping our words might signal their move.

Instead, our visitors responded: "Oh, that's all right. Never mind us; go right ahead."

When the young men did not budge, we realized they had been sent to oversee our packing. "We're in no hurry," we told them. "We are happy to chat."

Silence. Then the leader urged us to get to our task.

Throughout the day, shift after shift of youthful cadets came and went. They scrutinized everything we put into our trunks. At first they watched from the doorway. Step by step they ventured farther and farther into our rooms. They felt each piece of bedding, linen, and clothing as we folded it. Leafing through our books, they asked if we had maps or photos, discussing among themselves anything they questioned.

One particularly brash young man lifted my typewriter onto the table. Opening it, he told me to roll in a sheet of paper. He carefully pecked out, "I l-o-v-e y-o-u." Pleased with his efforts, he looked up for my approval.

"You type very well," I said.

Closing the machine, he said, "You'll not be allowed to take this." He took it to the room collecting the things we did not want or could not take.

We did not challenge their decisions, although they seemed to base those decisions on how an item took their fancy. The young typist confirmed our suspicion later in the afternoon when he retrieved the typewriter and returned it to me. "You may take this with you," he said sheepishly and disappeared. Elbow punching broke out among his fellows as he left. The cadets scrutinized our things less meticulously after that. In fact, they now urged us to complete our task quickly.

*P*acking had taken longer than anticipated, not only because of the surveillance, but because the authorities required detailed lists of the contents of each trunk. As we traveled, those lists would be checked against the items in our baggage again and again.

The sun was setting by the time we had finished our task. A senior officer arrived and, with a flourish, affixed his seal to the strips of rice paper pasted across the tops and over the latches and padlocks of our trunks. Broad strips of paper also sealed the doors to the room where the men had put the things we would leave behind.

After the police left, Dorothy and I attacked the

litter that remained. With a short-handled broom, I reached across one of the trunks to sweep behind it. I had barely touched the lid when it popped open, tearing the fragile seals. I gasped.

The trunk had not closed properly when the men pasted the paper seal across the stubborn latch. I had mentioned it, but they countered with, "Never mind—it's all right." Everyone's patience had worn thin by then, so I had not remonstrated. Now I regretted the fact as I stared at the torn seal. I called to Dorothy, "I'll have to go to report this."

Rain lashed my face as I hurried along the darkening streets. At the police station a stoic sentry challenged, "What is your business?"

"I wish to speak with someone who visited my house today," I told him. "I have come to report a broken seal."

"Wait here!" the guard said, then remained silent as he stood at attention in his shelter.

Waiting in the rain, I tried to find something to be thankful for as I watched my young "friends" inside enjoying their late meal. Hungry and thirsty, I sucked rain from my lips.

When the cadets finished eating and I had opportunity to explain my problem, an officer dispatched two reluctant men to look into the matter. Hurrying to keep up with the circle of light their lanterns cast about them, I followed. Back at our house, the two superficially examined the trunk, locked it properly, reapplied seals, and departed.

*U*tterly stressed out, I could not eat the supper Dorothy had left for me. Peeling off my muddy shoes and sodden clothing, I put on something dry and slid into my sleeping bag. Beneath me I felt the bare-rope bed, reminded that the mattress had been locked away in the sealed room. But I murmured a brief thanks to my heavenly Father for the trouble-free repair of the seal and slipped into oblivion with one final thought: *Will departure day ever really come?*

Dorothy and I spent the following day making quadruple copies of each trunk's "List of Contents" using my reclaimed typewriter. We translated them for Teacher Ho, who made identical lists in beautifully handwritten Chinese.

That evening Brother One surprised us with a visit to tell us a passenger boat bound for Chungking was expected in four days. We had not seen him for over a month. He had left our employment for another job when our activities—or rather inactivities—satisfied the authorities. His going relieved some of our financial problems, and preparing our own meals helped fill the days of waiting. We enjoyed seeing him again, though, and appreciated his continuing concern for our welfare.

The following morning a summons to assist with inoculations at the large middle school next door shattered our plans for a quiet Sunday.

As we entered one of the classrooms, screaming children fled, some jumping from windows six feet above the ground. Everyone found the experience painful. Teachers were embarrassed, children winced at the pricks, and the flashing hatred in young eyes that once danced to see us stung me. Months of cruel brain-washing had brought hurtful changes.

We wondered how we could be ready to leave the following day if asked again to help with inoculations. No one came to call us. Instead, we made the necessary trips to provincial, district, and local offices to "sign out" and turn in property deeds and keys.

At the Land Registration Office the official behind an imposing desk received us perfunctorily. Explaining our errand, Dorothy laid the deeds to mission property on his desk. Without reaching for the papers, he said, "The transfer of land in China is a very serious matter, you know. Ordinarily we could not receive these. But in view of your leaving our country, we will hold them until your return."

Our last trip was to collect our travel and exit permits at Provincial Police Headquarters. To our great surprise, we saw Walter Jespersen and Edith Jackson there, also preparing to leave China. In the few seconds we talked together before being separated, we learned we would be traveling together. What relief!—especially to have a man in our travel party! They had arrived in the city four days before but had not been allowed to visit or send word to us.

When the officer had completed and stamped our documents, he handed them to us. Courteously he showed us to the door and expressed regret at our going. Something in the officer's demeanor made me wonder if he was a brother in Christ. ■

‰16‱

Caught with Contraband!

O ur final evening in Luhsien Teacher Ho came to see that we had everything in order for our departure. While finishing preparations, I picked up a large handbag I planned to take for the journey. I had not used it in years. Opening it, I found, to my dismay, six dimes and a U.S. two-dollar bill I had completely forgotten.

Ho-Ho stared at the bill. "Well!" she exclaimed, "you will have to get rid of *that* before morning. You know it should have been turned in months ago."

"I know," I said soberly. "I'll burn it in the morning."

Teacher Ho left about midnight. Slipping my hand into hers, I gave it a squeeze and with a kiss whispered in her ear, "I wish I could take you with me."

With moist eyes, Ho-Ho looked into mine, shook her head, and, turning, went down the steps.

The next morning I eagerly pushed back the pre-dawn darkness with my small flashlight and crawled from my sleeping bag. While dressing, I discerned the familiar figures of Teacher Ho, Pastor Philip, Andrew, and Anna moving around the small charcoal stoves behind Teacher Ho's room. I wondered how early they had begun breakfast preparations. They had invited Dorothy and me to a farewell meal at seven-thirty. We knew it would be a tasty breakfast.

My throat tightened at the thought of leaving. *I'll see them in Heaven, but will I ever see them down here again?*

I stood watching the activity for a few moments, then lit the lamp and picked up my little devotional book of Scripture, *Daily Light on the Daily Path.* I turned to May 30. The last words in that morning's portion seized my attention. "The Lord shall be unto thee an everlasting light and thy God thy glory" (Is. 60:19, KJV). Tears came as I pondered God's promise and thought about the futures my friends and I faced. We had passed through some perilous times together. More would follow. I knew the promise was as true for those staying as for those of us leaving. Our friends would, no doubt, experience the greater trials.

Shuffling feet on the path outside alerted me to someone's presence. I went to the window. Brother One stood there looking up and holding a small lighted faggot in one hand. "Something for your breakfast," he called. He held up a small parcel in his free hand.

I went outside to receive the warm bag, made from a copy sheet of some child's exercise book. I peeked inside at warm sweet rolls. "Oh, thank you, Brother One," I said, bowing.

Turning to leave, he said, "I must go to the market now, but I'll return at nine o'clock to rope up your trunks and take them to the boat for you."

Going back to my room, I prayed for the young man, asking that he would live in God's light and seek to glorify Him.

Dorothy and I each munched on a delicious roll while doing up our hand luggage. Everything was coming together nicely by the time we received the call for breakfast.

Spread on Teacher Ho's table lay a feast of love. Over that table we spent a comfortable, relaxed hour. The Lord was very near as we encouraged one another with promises from His Word. I shared my early-morning gem.

When time came to go, the two men explained they would not go with us to the wharf. "It seems wiser," they said.

"But we'll go with you," promised Ho-Ho and Anna.

Hurrying outside, our hearts tight with the pain of parting, we found Brother One and his friends ready to rope up our baggage. They had only begun their work when twelve soldiers burst into the courtyard. We stared, wondering. "Open those trunks!" one of the soldiers commanded.

With quaking hearts, we replied, "Oh, but we can't do that! The police sealed them three days ago." We pointed to the official red stamps on the paper seals.

"Open them!" the leader of the band shouted.

Trying to explain only nettled the man. Vexed by our refusal to comply, the soldiers slit the seals with their bayonets. "Now," the leader commanded, "unlock them!"

Dorothy and I each opened a trunk. The offended soldiers rummaged through the contents. When they had shaken out and tossed every item from the two trunks onto the ground, they turned to another. "Open that one!" they snapped, pointing to my second trunk.

"Sir, I cannot do that until I have repacked this one," I protested, "lest things get mixed up. Then our 'contents lists' would be incorrect."

Impatiently two men lent a hand. The lid would not close. While the agitated soldiers watched, I lifted the contents from the trunk. Carefully refolding each item, I repacked it and closed the lid. The search through the second trunk was cursory.

During that tense hour I remembered the money I had neglected to destroy. While the soldiers finished Dorothy's trunks, I excused myself and went up to my room. Snatching up the two-dollar bill, I stuffed it into my gown. Hearing footsteps on the stairs I looked for a crack between the floor boards through which to drop the dimes. I was too late; the bold intruders came right into my room.

"What are you doing?" they asked suspiciously.

"A little last-minute packing," I replied. "Our boat is due soon."

The soldiers looked about the room and spotted the coins on my desk. "What are those?" they demanded.

"A little American money," I answered as casually as my pounding heart would allow.

"How much is it worth in our money?" they wanted to know.

After rapid calculation, I answered, "Several hundred yuan."

"Didn't you know it's against the law to have American money?" They spat the words at me with derision.

Other "comrades" now crowded in. Dorothy, trembling, followed them into the room. "It's the money," I said quietly.

With a charge against me now, the soldiers whooped, "To the police station with you!"

I grabbed at my bag as an angry soldier swept his arm across my desk, scattering everything left there. Scrambling to the floor for my exit permit, passport, and travel money, I was reaching for my Bible, when a second command, "Go!" resounded.

Gathering up what we could, Dorothy and I stumbled out the door and down the steps with pressuring soldiers close behind us. When they saw that Brother One and the carriers had gone with our trunks, they swore. Obviously they had designs of their own for those goods.

Teacher Ho and Anna stood in their doorway, silent. I glanced their way without a word or expression that could implicate them and left the old compound.

Outside, the curious had gathered to see what was happening to the foreigners. Over-zealous young soldiers flourishing their weapons prodded us along the street. At the intersection to a local police sub-station, I turned. A bayonet jabbed at my back. "Where do you think you're going?" someone yelled.

"To the police station," I replied.

"Not this one. You're going to the Provincial Headquarters uptown."

We turned back onto the main street. Inwardly I breathed a sign of relief. We had received our travel documents at Provincial Headquarters the evening before. The officials there were not boys. Remembering the courteous officer, I prayed, *Lord, please send Your angel before us!*

We certainly created a spectacle as we left our neighborhood with twelve soldiers and bayonets at our backs. By the end of our forced march through the city we scarcely drew a glance. Only two adolescent soldiers, their guns now shouldered, still followed us.

Our youthful captors seemed at a loss to explain our presence to the guard outside the police headquarters. They released us to him and hurried away. The guard led us to the building we had visited the previous day. The courteous officer we had met before appeared surprised to see us. "What brings you back?" he asked.

I explained about the dimes.

"How much money have you?" was his next query.

I laid six coins on his desk. Looking at his watch, he spoke, "Your boat leaves soon, doesn't it?"

"That's correct," I replied.

"You will need to write a confession," he said, pushing a sheet of paper and writing equipment toward me.

"Though I write a little Chinese character, I am not competent to compose such a document," I responded.

The officer got up from his desk. "Wait here!" he said and left the room.

Through what seemed one of the longest waits of my life, I wondered if my exit permit would be canceled. In the midst of those torturing thoughts, however, I found a place where my "thanksgiving key" would fit. *Thank You, Lord, for a quiet room where no one is shouting at me.*

The officer returned thirty-five minutes later with a carefully written legal paper. "Sign here, then you may go," he said.

I hesitated, wondering if I had heard correctly. "Sign here," he repeated, pointing to a space at the lower left corner.

Without reading my confession, I signed it!

"That is all," he said quietly.

Close to tears, I thanked him simply, then added, "God bless you, sir."

Again with a slight nod, the man turned and escorted us to the door. Surely he was God's angel!

Silently jubilant and truly thankful, Dorothy and I left the building. Though Dorothy had a final errand at the post office, I went directly to the inn to find our fellow-missionary travelers. Barely acknowledging their greeting or the babble of their excited children, I begged to go to their sleeping quarters. In its seclusion I burst into tears.

M inutes later I heard Teacher Ho's voice. She entered the room, sat down on the bed beside me, and laid her hand gently on my convulsing shoulder. "Whatever happened this morning?" she asked.

Between sobs I told her about the sixty cents. "I told you to get rid of that money," she chided.

"Yes, I know, but I forgot to do it before we came to breakfast." Then I added, "But how did you get here?"

"I waited until the furor died down before I left the compound," she said. "I took the west road that goes outside the wall through the country and came back around through east gate. Anna came another way. She's outside. We had to know what happened."

Our friends called from the outer room, "We hear the boat whistle! That means we can buy our tickets."

Teacher Ho got up. "By the way, what about the two-dollar bill?"

"It's here," I said, touching the front of my gown. "I'll throw it into the river when we get going."

"What!" she exclaimed. "You still have that bill? Don't you know that you'll be searched when you go onto the boat? Give it to me!"

I handed Ho-Ho the crumpled bill. As she left the room, I noticed that she limped more than usual.

We went to the ticket office to purchase our tickets,

Caught with Contraband!

then returned to the inn to collect personal things before leaving for the boat. A long flight of temporary wooden steps stretched to the shallow river. Picking my way carefully down them, I suddenly realized that Ho-Ho was at my elbow. "Ho-Ho," I said, "did you get rid of it?"

Ho-Ho nodded.

"Did you burn it?" I asked anxiously.

She shook her head.

"You didn't give it to anyone?

Again she shook her head no.

"What *did* you do with it?" I asked.

Her non-verbal reply was to show me the tip of her tongue with the last tiny piece of the two-dollar bill on it.

"Oh, but it couldn't have tasted good!" I exclaimed.

She shook her head vigorously. "No, it wasn't a very tasty snack," she admitted with a wry smile.

Other passengers crowded to get past us on the narrow steps.

"Thank you, thank you, beloved teacher," I whispered, and turned away.

Teacher Ho limped back up the steps to join Anna and Brother One on the high bank. We boarded the boat and found the baggage Brother One had deposited in our cabins, then returned to stand by the rail and wave goodbye.

I saw Teacher Ho turn to Brother One. He pivoted and disappeared into the crowd. Reappearing shortly, he brought two paper bags to the wharf. "Teacher Ho thought the children might get hungry before next meal time," he called as he deposited the bags with the steward. Inside them we found fourteen sweet mooncakes. The loving, sacrificial gift touched us deeply. I was glad to have been included among "the children."

The loyal three stayed on the riverbank until we lifted anchor about two-thirty p.m. We responded to their flutter of large handkerchiefs until a bend in the river separated us from view.

One day I shall look for the welcoming flutter of handkerchiefs (or their counterpart) on another shore. Teacher Ho, at least, has already gone on ahead. When Ron and Gwen Roberts, my first senior workers at Luhsien, returned as tourists to visit West Sichuan in 1980, they learned that she had been struck by a moving truck about a year prior to their visit. She was killed instantly.

Dear Ho-Ho—"with Christ, which is far better." ■

෨17෬

Road to Freedom

Running with the current, the unpretentious steamer carried us swiftly away from the true friends we had left behind. The painful parting still weighed on my heart.

Yet traveling with missionary companions we had not seen for nearly two years helped ease the pain and lifted my spirits. We forgot time as we exchanged tales of eventful days and months just past.

Twenty-four hours after leaving Luhsien we reached Chungking. There we had to finalize exit formalities and travel arrangements. While seemingly endless hours of interrogation strained our patience, the fellowship of friends and knowing we were on our way to freedom buoyed us.

After eighteen days at Chungking authorities permitted us to travel on. We procured passage on a small shallow-draft freighter that could traverse the treacherous Yangtze Gorge rapids in low-water season. Six of our party faced the journey in the windowless-and-portholeless hold of the overloaded boat. A single dim light held back the darkness. By boarding early, however, we secured a place for our bedrolls near one of the loading hatches. There an occasional breeze from outside freshened the dank air.

The recent interrogations had so emotionally and physically drained us that we hardly minded when people stumbled over or around us—whether carriers loading coal or other passengers coming to share our quarters.

Fortunately, Helen Jespersen and her four children found quarters above. Lest we lose our choice spot by the hatch, we did not go up to see them often. Much of that two-and-a-half-day trip we slept, missing most of the world-famous gorges. What we did see from our water-level hatch—mountains rearing straight up from surging rapids—was marred by the sight of corpses churning in the rapids. Finally the choked river burst from its rocky confines onto a broad plain.

*E*ventually the freighter carried us to a sprawling city where we expected to transfer to a passenger boat. None of us suspected the misery that awaited us.

As people who needed "special handling," we were last off the freighter. Ferried to the river's edge, we waited with a group of fourteen nuns and a priest until all baggage had come ashore.

That accomplished, authorities handed us over to an evil innkeeper who refused to permit us outside the filthy inn for any reason. Virtually prisoners, we were forced to depend on the man for every need.

When one of the Jespersen children developed diarrhea, the nuns, with whom our captors had forbidden us to communicate, slipped Walter medicine that no doubt saved the child's life.

Daily we heard boat whistles, but the innkeeper insisted no space was available on them. By postponing our departure, the unscrupulous man combed in handsome fees from twenty-six unwilling guests.

Each day we carried our clothing and bedding to the flat roof of the inn to search out and crush hundreds of bedbugs crowding seams and folds. I doubt the proprietor appreciated our assistance in depleting the hotel's bedbug population, but it gave us something to do.

We shall never know how long we might have remained there had a Chinese guest at the inn not spoken to Walter. "They have no right to keep you here," he whispered. "A steamer went out empty this morning. Another will leave tomorrow." With his finger he traced a cross on the palm of his hand and hurried on down the steps.

Prompted by that bit of information, the men in our party demanded to go out to see for themselves. Reluctantly the proprietor agreed to "go again and check." He returned with tickets for all, at one-and-a-half times the regular fare. He did not release us until sunset—after another expensive meal! Rain was falling heavily when he shouted, "Now go! Get out!"

Leaders in our group had asked for rickshaws to take some of the elderly, crippled nuns to the wharf.

When only two rickshaws came, the innkeeper insisted they bear the mother of the sick child and the person carrying the six-month-old infant—me! I felt indignation and shame as we rode past the older women sloshing painfully along the darkening streets.

The river steamer seemed from another world—and indeed it was! The luxury ship we found at the pier had once belonged to a Dutch company. Welcomed aboard the spacious, well-lit vessel, we found the drastic change in our circumstances almost bewildering. Ample, clean cabins and warm water for bathing, like balm, helped soothe the strain of the previous days.

The next day the steamer decks looked much like a laundry yard as we washed and hung our things to dry on lines rigged by a helpful steward. The ship had carried other detainees from the infamous city before us. Some, crew members told us, had been held for three weeks.

For two nights and a day, as we steamed through central China, we enjoyed tender tokens of our Father's love.

At Hankow, the junction of the Yangtze River and the state-run Southern Railroad, we spent a full day. During the grueling inspection one of the Jespersen children, a blond five-year-old in a blue sunbonnet, climbed atop a pile of luggage and broke into song. Her choice of music? A communist propaganda song learned from cadets practicing on the badminton court at her home in west China! Soldiers and police gathered around and applauded heartily. After that the authorities seemed less intrusive.

In the evening we boarded a comfortable train for another two-and-a-half day journey to Canton, where travel agents (actually plain-clothes policemen) met us and assisted us to a hotel. The next morning they woke us early and hustled us back to the train station for another baggage examination.

At the end of another five hours on the train we found ourselves sweltering in a tin-roofed shed only yards from China's border with the Hong Kong Territories. There we underwent our third frisk and eighth and most thorough baggage "turn out." Afterwards, as we gathered up our scattered possessions, we cast wistful eyes toward a huge British flag, the "Union Jack," fluttering beyond the barbed-wire barrier.

While the travel agents oversaw the repacked baggage across the border, the Jespersens, Edith, and two Swiss workers moved through the barricade. Still on the China side, I walked behind Dorothy toward the same portal to freedom, where we would surrender our travel passes and exit permits. At the gate Dorothy frantically searched for her documents. They *had* been in her bag! Utterly disconcerted, we heard one of the guards say, "You must go back." Every ounce of energy drained from me.

Dorothy could neither have boarded the train in Canton nor come into the examination shed without a pass. Where could those documents have gone?

Beyond the barrier Walter, hearing and seeing the growing commotion, stepped back to the gate. As Dorothy explained her dilemma to him, a guard broke in. "She must go back to Chungking," he said sternly.

"Would you allow her to go and see if the papers are in her baggage that has gone ahead?" Walter asked. "It's just over there." He pointed to the pile of jumbled boxes and trunks on the Hong Kong side.

"No!" came the curt reply.

"If I cross back to China's side and stand in her place," asked Walter, "would you allow her to go with the travel agent to look for it?"

To this the border guards agreed.

I waited, still on China's soil, clutching my all-important papers securely. I prayed that Dorothy would quickly find hers and thanked the Lord for a family man who unselfishly volunteered to stand in for a single co-worker.

Dorothy returned waving the precious documents. She had put them into another of her bags. Once she handed the permits to the unsmiling guard, she and Walter turned toward the border. Numb with apprehension, I surrendered my travel pass and exit permit and walked through the small gate in the barbed-wire barrier.

All I now wanted was to distance myself from the border. Resisting a strong impulse to run, I followed the footpath that led away from that gate.

Hong Kong police in spotless uniforms and gleaming boots stepped forward. "This way, Teachers," they directed politely, indicating the immigration building below the huge Union Jack. I saw the rippling flag quiver in the breeze. My heart did the same as tears welled up in my eyes..

The solemn faces of officers relaxed into smiles. They had witnessed the exchanges at the border. "You can be glad you found your papers," one of them told Dorothy. "We've recently seen two others sent back from that gate. They have not returned."

Staring back at the narrow portal through which we had just passed, I shuddered. "It's all right. You're safe now," comforted an observant officer. "You can't be taken back from here."

*I*nside Immigration, officials hastily examined and stamped our passports, then hustled us off to the train that waited for us. Leaning from open windows, passengers cheered as the two of us climbed aboard. We had no sooner found our seats than from some-where in the coach a tremulous voice started to sing The Doxology. In several languages "Praise God from whom all blessings flow" sprang spontaneously from hearts filled with gratitude and, like wild fire, spread from car to car.

For us and others like us that day—July 29, 1951— became Freedom Day.

Savoring liberty, I thought of the past months and whispered a tearful thanks to God. *Oh, Lord,* I prayed silently, *I have so much yet to learn. Will You teach me about giving thanks in the hard places too?*

Vendors in the aisle interrupted my reverie with shouts of, "Apples! Oranges! Chocolate! Ice-cold soda!" Drawing from my purse the last of my Chinese currency, I squandered every last *yuan* on those incredible luxuries.

Friends met our travel-weary party at Hong Kong's Kowloon station and drove us to a cluster of bayside Quonset huts our mission had rented from the government as a temporary evacuation center. Fellow evacuees cheerfully pushed their cots and meager belongings closer together to make room for us. Though still bewildered, I quickly felt the solace of those who understood and cared. After introductions and dinner in the mess hall we gathered under the stars to worship and pray for fellow missionaries still detained in China.

Agents obtained steamer passage for Dorothy the very next day. I sailed for America a week later via the Suez Canal and England. ■

ಎ18ಞ

Pursuing the Promise

With tears of joy, open arms and hearty hugs, friends and family received me home. Invariably my greeters followed their welcome with, "Well, Mary, now that you're back, what do you plan to do?"

I honestly did not know.

"You can be as effective a missionary right here at home as in China, you know," people would say. "There are great needs here also." Or, "Since you are a qualified nurse, lots of good positions with good pay are out there waiting for you." The most helpful would add, "I know just the job for you. Let me get you an application."

After years of restraint in Communist China, I struggled to readjust to outspoken America. Awash in the abundance of "good" advice and suggestions, I felt as if I were swimming against the tide in a syrupy sea. More than anything, I wanted to know God's will for my life and to fulfill my early promise to Him. Once again I felt like an alien, this time in my own country.

The first few months after my return from China provided time for soul-searching. Looking back, I saw the wisdom and love of my heavenly Father in allowing every testing. While I had done virtually nothing *for* Christ during my China years, He had used the storms as discipline to train and shape me for His purposes. I knew that His clear call to me had not changed. Neither had my promise to Him. The assurance of my heavenly Father's continued hand on my life prepared me to return to Asia.

In the meantime, as the doors to China closed, the leadership of the China Inland Mission (later Overseas Missionary Fellowship or OMF) earnestly sought the Lord's direction for the future and had already begun assigning missionaries to work among the countless Chinese living in the countries around China. I wanted to join them. After nine months in the States I wrote to the new headquarters in Singapore, offering to serve anywhere I could fill a need.

The day after my arrival in Singapore, Arnold Lea, one of the mission's directors, interviewed me. In his small office the broad blades of a ceiling fan stirred the hot, humid air. Mr. Lea surprised me by inquiring about Teacher Ho. He had, I discovered, spent his first years in China living in Luhsien. His genuine concern for our mutual friend put me at ease.

"Mary, do you like nursing?" my interviewer asked, changing the subject.

My immediate "yes" brought a smile to his face.

His second question, "Do you like institutional nursing?" received a similar answer.

"Good!" he said. "Many nurses, after arriving on the field, prefer other ministries." He paused, then continued. "Today we received a communiqué from Thailand's Minister of Health in response to our inquiry about medical needs there. He has invited our cooperation in their rural health program." Watching carefully for my reaction, he went on. "In view of your open offer to serve in any field, would you consider Thailand?"

Before I could respond he spoke again, "Don't answer now," he said. "Let's pray about it first. Come again at two tomorrow afternoon." He rose and extended his hand.

I went to the room where I was staying and prayed: *Lord, You know the need. You know me. Please lead me to that place where You can best use me. Did You time that letter from Thailand to come today so that we would know Your way, Lord?*

I knew very little about Thailand, the tiny Buddhist kingdom that lay to the south of China. I knew even less about the Thai people. But when I rose from prayer, I had a quiet peace in my heart—I knew God was leading me to Thailand.

The next day Mr. Lea and I rejoiced at the Lord's perfectly timed guidance.

"Before you go to Thailand, Mary," Mr. Lea added, "would you be willing to give a hand in Malaya? Several of our missionaries there need vacations.

Could you go for a few weeks to give them a break?"
    I agreed to go.

So, for a second time, I moved into a country
fomenting with communism. In 1953 Malaya was
at the height of her national emergency. Bands of
leftist guerrillas prowled the countryside, threatening
the peninsula's future. Government forces fought
back. On top of a strict dusk-to-dawn curfew, no one
could travel anywhere except in convoy with military
escort. The ever-present soldiers, though not hostile to
us, brought back haunting memories and triggered
fears I had to commit to the Lord.

    For my first five-week assignment I went to a
detention camp a few miles north of Singapore. There
the commandant asked me to teach mathematics and
Bible to children. The bright-eyed youngsters, along
with their parents, awaited deportation back to China
because of pro-communist activities. While that teaching assignment demanded a quick recall of my scant
Chinese language, I enjoyed it.

    When that assignment ended, I worked in primary
health-care clinics and helped with evangelistic out-
reaches to women and children in three "New Villages." The Malayan government had laid out and
built hundreds of these New Villages in a gigantic
effort to halt communism. A high perimeter fence,
complete with guard towers, surrounded each village.
People from jungle-clad mountains to the plains were
uprooted from their homes and resettled within those
perimeters.

Though the uprooting gave security from raiders, people found confinement in hot, treeless villages incredibly taxing. But for Christian workers this dislocation and resettlement opened a door to share the message of the love and compassion of Christ. Most New Village people had never heard the name of Jesus. Living and working among them often seemed like being in old China.

*T*hough I could have continued happily among Malaya's uprooted Chinese, an urgent telegram changed my life once again. It read: "PROCEED IMMEDIATELY TO THAILAND STOP APPLY TO SIT GOVERNMENT NURSE REGISTRATION EXAM IN TWO WEEKS STOP."

Collecting my things, I flew to Bangkok and unimagined changes. As our plane approached Thailand's fabled capital, the gilded rooftops of a hundred Buddhist temples glistened in the afternoon sun. When I deplaned at Bangkok's international airport, heat rose off the tarmac like the fury of a gigantic furnace. Once through immigration and customs, I went outside to wait for a limousine that would take me into the city.

The unfamiliar flowed all around me—faces, dress, the language, and the strange script on signs.

I felt a heaviness I blamed on the heat and the excitement of arrival. In the days that followed I would learn the real source of that heaviness.

The airport limousine filled quickly for the twelve-mile drive into the city. A friend met me at the air office and arranged transport across Bangkok in a motorized two-passenger tricycle. On that first wild ride in one of the city's *tup-tups*, we zigzagged through congested streets and putt-putted down narrow lanes, finally arriving safely at the mission house.

After a cool drink the mission home hostess led me from the airy, Thai-style house to a dark, three-story building behind it. I followed her up unsheltered, outside steps that swayed beneath our tread. In a small room on the top floor she pushed a chair under a tiny desk to make room for my suitcases. "This was once a sausage factory," she said laughingly. "That's what we still call it because we really are squeezed in!" Turning to go, she added, "The bathroom is on the ground floor. Supper will be ready soon." Over her shoulder she flung, "You'll hear the gong."

When she had gone, I sat down on the board bed padded with a thin kapok mattress. As I surveyed the airless room, I understood why I had seen so many fan shops on the way from the airport!

As I had left my heavy luggage to follow me by ship from Singapore, unpacking did not take long. The next day—after shopping for a fan—I began reviewing for the nursing exam and studying the Thai language.

My language teacher, an older woman, was half German and half Thai-Chinese. She reminded me of Ho-Ho.

Like Chinese, spoken Thai is tonal. Even so, I found it very different. In Thai the length given to a vowel is as important to the meaning of a word as its tone. To my ears all vowels sounded short.

One day I remarked to my teacher about the dull heaviness I had felt since the day of my arrival. Her gentle reply enlightened me. "You probably feel that way because of the oppressive forces of evil that hold sway in our land. Don't be discouraged, but keep very close to the Lord Jesus Christ." I never forgot her wise counsel.

Instead of two weeks the nurse registration exams took place two-and-a-half *months* after my hurried trip from Malaya. During that period I learned well the meaning of an oft-used Thai word, *dee-oo*. Freely translated, it means "soon." That may mean a minute, an hour, a week, or even a few months. The delay in the exam, however, did give me extra time for nursing review. When I finally took the three-day written and oral exam, I passed and received my Thai nursing certificate.

I expected to find Thailand similar to Malaya. But unlike Malaya, Thailand had never been colonized by the West. She remained herself—purely East. About the turn of the century the country changed her name from Siam to Thailand—"Land of the Free"—a name she still bears proudly.

After a short stay in upcountry Thailand, substituting for a fellow-worker, I went to live in a provincial city on the banks of Thailand's largest river, about a hundred miles north of Bangkok. I shared an old-style Thai house on stilts with Ralph and Sheilah

Willecome, a young English couple assigned to church
planting and Ruth Metcalf, an Australian nurse. All
four of us newcomers to the land, we had much to
learn as we began to put down roots in central Thailand's rice-growing plains.

In spite of the language barrier, I enjoyed the
warmth of our Thai neighbors' welcoming smiles. I
watched with fascination as the grandpa and grandma
next door pounded out the family's daily ration of rice.
Using long-handled hardwood mallets in turn, they
alternated with perfect coordination, loosening the
husks from the grain in a hollowed-out log. When the
hulls had separated from the rice, the old woman
deftly tossed the mixture into the air from a large,
shallow tray. Wind carried the husks away. *How like
Bible times!* I thought.

The river's edge at the front of our rented house
bustled with activity. I enjoyed watching neighbors
weed or water their small garden patches on the
fertile riverbank. Herds of mud-encrusted water buffalo kicked up clouds of dust as they lumbered down
gullied paths before plunging into the water. There
the docile creatures puffed and snorted as their owners scrubbed them down with coconut bark.

Families came to the river together for their
evening baths. Children frolicking in the water always
brought a smile to my face. They were usually still
dancing when their mothers corralled them to soap
them down. When they finished their baths, the bare-
bodied youngsters scampered off to resume their play.
Adults modestly pulled up fresh long, dry skirts, knot-

ting them securely across their chests before loosing and stepping out of wet ones. Each bather then returned to the shallows to launder the clothing that they had just removed.

Our neighbors repeatedly invited us to join them. Each time we declined they shook their heads, puzzling at why we would continue lugging heavy buckets of water up to our house instead of bathing and doing our laundry in the river—the easy way!

In that provincial city I learned about the ubiquitous Thai giggle, a safe and culturally acceptable smoke-screen in any I-don't-know-what-to-do situation—their way of relieving embarrassment.

The neighborhood children had their share of cuts, scratches, insect bites, and burns. We told their mothers we had medicines that might bring healing more quickly. Thus began a nightly after-bath paint-and-plaster clinic. Evening after evening our verandah overflowed with chattering youngsters searching arms or legs for a scratch or bite that might earn a dab of gentian violet or a bit of gauze and adhesive tape. Not infrequently we would see a child pick off a scab just to get coveted attention!

The children loved the scrapbooks we laid out for them. Older ones proudly demonstrated superior ability by loudly reading the Bible verses we had printed at the top of a page or under a picture. Those nightly frolics were forerunners of a Bible story hour.

When word spread that three of the foreigners now living in the lawyer's rented house were nurses, mothers began bringing babies with infected eyes or

ears. Others came with cuts that called for stitches or
teeth that needed extracting. Those with more serious
problems we referred to medical facilities in Bangkok,
over a hundred miles away. We began to understand
why the government had invited our mission to assist
with health care in rural Thailand.

We chose the weeks just prior to Christmas to
begin sharing the good news of Jesus on a
wider scale. Day after day, our baskets full of gospel
literature, we followed early morning shoppers to the
open market. A colorful Christmas storybook and
inexpensive packets of Scripture sold quickly. As curious, amiable people crowded about us, I felt keenly
my inability to respond to friendly questions.

At the end of each book-selling day we asked God
to use His Word, now in the hands of people who had
probably never had it before.

As Christmas Day drew near, we pinned bright
cards sent by our overseas friends to our flannelgraph
board. From the ceiling we hung a gold star. A couple
of silver streamers completed our decorations. For
neighborhood children we made popcorn balls, tag-
ging each with a pretty card. For adults we made
fudge to give with a Christmas tract.

Christmas Eve I took a blanket to the verandah and
lay alone for a time looking up into the starry sky. A
soft murmur of voices wafted from nearby homes.
Though I felt a tinge of nostalgia as I thought of other
Christmases, I was glad to be right where I was.

Christmas morning the strains of *Christian, Awake!*

Greet This Happy Morn! broke into the stillness. I sat up, wondering! Through mosquito netting and the screen door I saw Ralph and Sheilah sitting on the verandah beside my little battery-operated phonograph. Slipping into my dressing gown, I went to join them just as Ruthie emerged from her room. Together we watched the first glimmer of dawn appear, then glow above the dark outlines of a Buddhist temple on the far riverbank. As the phonograph head, with a gentle bobbing motion, followed the grooves on the black disks, we sang along. Though the little instrument produced less than high-fidelity music, I thrilled to the words of *I Know that My Redeemer Liveth* from Handel's *Messiah*.

Suddenly Ruthie exclaimed, "Oh, look!" She pointed to the south. There, low in the sky, above silhouetted palm trees, hung a constellation the three

of us from England and America had never seen—the Southern Cross. That Christmas morning we worshiped in God's own cathedral, reminded again of our reason for coming to Thailand. ■

ꙮ19ꙮ
A New Direction

After the New Year we settled into more scheduled routines. We engaged teachers from the primary school on the temple grounds across the river to help us learn Thai in their off hours. As they had other commitments on Thursdays, we set that day aside for regular literature distribution.

I found myself dreading Thursdays. Invariably I awakened with a headache. Excuses by the dozen tumbled through my head: *It's too hot, too cold, too wet, or too windy to go out today. Stay home and get on with language study. You need that! Besides, you're not a salesperson. It won't hurt to miss just this one time.*

I began to understand the words of my Bangkok teacher about the "powers of darkness." The living Word of God now challenged those powers. Obviously they opposed our literature-distribution forays into the countryside.

We always prayed for protection and the enabling

of God's Spirit before we went out. Usually my part-
ner and I had barely descended the steps and exited
the front gate before my headache disappeared.

Much of my conflict came from fear of failure. By
choosing obedience to the Lord over my fears, I
discovered that once I had offered the literature, fear
vanished, and I enjoyed the contact. Language ability
grew as well.

Barking watchdogs or honking "watch geese" usually announced our approach to a home. As a rule, the
grandmother of the home emerged from work under
the house on stilts. Or she rose from where she lay,
cooing softly to a sleeping child in a homemade ham-
mock. Dogs would usually slink away at her command. The geese would persist until, in response to an
invitation to "come and sit awhile," we were at the
granny's side.

The older woman, gently stroking our hands,
would remark how white and soft they were. She then
questioned us, kindly correcting our mispronounced
words as she would correct a child. "Where have you
come from?" she might ask. "Do you like our country?
How many children do you have? You're not married?! But how old are you? Did your government
send you? How much money do you make?"

After the inevitable questions, we could tell her the
real reason for our visit. "We've come to bring you
books with words from the God in Heaven."

The most common response was, "I can't read
books, but I have a grandson who can—he's been to
school." So saying, she would draw a few small coins

from a little pocket at the front of her loose-fitting blouse or from the tucked-in upper part of her long, straight skirt. Usually she bought the books without question.

One day Ruthie and I planned to visit an upriver market about an hour's boat ride away. Because we had never gone there before and because literature usually sold quicker in new places, we took a larger than usual quantity of tract sets and Scripture booklets. Arriving at our destination, we found upturned tables, benches, and empty stalls. It was not market day! In addition, the boatman told us not expect any downriver boats until late afternoon. No boat meant we would have to lug the literature home.

We began our homeward trek, stopping at each riverside home. At the gateway to one large farmyard a man came to greet us. He bought a set of Scriptures, then looked through our baskets for other booklets. *May he buy lots,* I thought, *so these baskets won't be so heavy!* So much for good motives!

While the man searched through my basket, I saw beyond him a youth obviously trying to hide behind a sturdy post that supported a rice granary. As we turned to go, I smiled at the boy. We had gone only a few paces when our customer called us back. "I'd like another set of your books, please," he said, "and different free literature too."

We retraced our steps. Again I saw the youth retreating toward the granary. It was he who wanted the second set of books. From a safe distance he turned and smiled through thick, swollen lips. The nurse in me wanted to go to him. He looked like pictures I had seen of people with Hansen's disease, commonly known as leprosy. Though I could do nothing for him, I asked God to use the Word he had just purchased. I prayed, too, that our medical program might soon get underway.

The smile on that prematurely aged and misshapen face haunted me. Contact with that afflicted young man foreshadowed things to come. I little imagined how quickly God would answer my prayer.

A few evenings later the four of us sat relaxing on our sheltered verandah when we heard the approach of visitors. Ralph went to welcome the two men who stood at the foot of the stairs. One he did not recognize. The other, a teacher who lived a few houses away, was the father of children who often came to our house. After the usual small talk the teacher said, "My friend, Tube, asked me to come with him tonight. He wonders if you can help him."

We turned our eyes to the younger man. He hesitated a moment, then explained shyly that he'd never been to school. "But," he said, "I am learning English by listening to The Voice of America."

He shifted uneasily. I expected his next words would be a request for English lessons. Instead, slowly, carefully, he repeated a well-practiced English sentence, spelling out the last word, "I have l-e-p-r-o-s-y." Searching our faces, he paused, then cautiously held out a crippled hand.

I took his deformed hand in mine to examine it. "I do not have medicine for your disease," I told him, "but we have a friend who lives a day's journey upriver who has just the medicine that could help you."

Disappointment showed on his face. A week later he came to tell us he had visited my friend. "The nurse was very kind," he said. "She gave me medicine and told me to come to you if it made me sick. Do you mind?" he asked.

Wondering what we would do if he got sick from the medicine, I replied, "I'm happy to help as I'm able."

"Then you don't despise me?" he asked earnestly. "Everyone says I must have done something terrible in a former life to be like this. I just can't remember what it was," he concluded sadly.

He spoke quickly, and many of the terms he used we did not understand. I went for my dictionary. He had told us that because he was only seven when they discovered his disease, the community had not allowed him in school. We found, however, that he could read very well. With his help, and that of his friend, we located in the dictionary the Buddhist terms and Thai idioms he had used.

We tried to explain that his disease did not result from sin in a former incarnation, but, as with many diseases, from the invasion into the body of creatures too small to see without a microscope.

"I don't go out like this except at night because people are afraid of me. They know what I have because of this——" He pointed to his dropped foot. "They laugh at me, call me names, and spit at me. They all say I deserve what I have and should be ashamed. I'm trying to live a good life and to make enough merit to outweigh my evil so that in my next life I won't be like this."

With limited language, we tried to tell him about the God who loved and cared for him. We gave him a New Testament and another book to help him understand God's love.

A couple of weeks later Tube returned. This time he had a high fever and suffered from severe pain. "I felt better after I began taking the medicine," he explained, "so I thought I would get better even faster if I took it more quickly."

The lad had taken his whole two-month supply in two and a half weeks! I saw for the first time a severe leprosy-medicine reaction. We all felt deep concern as we sat together listening to his distressing symptoms. I wondered what to do.

A gusty wind blew out our kerosene lamp for the third time. Because a full moon softened the darkness, we did not bother to relight it. When I rose to go for pain medicine, I noticed the teen-age son of our landlord standing in the shadows at the top of our stairs. He gestured to someone below. Seeing me, he retreated.

In that moment a storm of ugly words erupted under our house. We recognized the voice of our landlord. Though we did not understand much of what he shouted, Tube understood. The drunken man soundly cursed the youth and ordered him from our home. The young man turned a stricken face toward us. Rising, he said, "I must go." Then in English he said, "Sorry! Sorry!"

The inebriated man continued the abusive tirade until one of his wives led him away. Stunned, we watched our patient limp silently down the steps and disappear into the darkness. We did not know where he lived, so could not go to him that night, but we prayed earnestly for him.

The next morning, hearing a sharp exchange of words at the landlord's house, I looked out. The youth's mother had come to ask for an explanation of the previous night's confrontation. The landlord, though now sober, stoutly declared he did not know who had been at the foreigner's house. "I was only trying to protect them," he protested.

No explanation was needed by any who heard the abuse. At one time or another, most people in the community had felt the sting of that vicious tongue. Throughout the morning neighbors came to express regret over the affair. Though a nasty episode, it gave us opportunity to explain that we did not despise people with leprosy. "Our God enables us to forgive those who offend us because He has forgiven *us*," we told our visitors. Our neighbors nodded thoughtfully, then acknowledged, "We're not like that. We hold grudges for life."

Ralph discovered where Tube lived and took the medicines we'd been unable to give the night before.

Later that morning our househelper said, "Did you

know that Tube, after leaving here last night, went straight to the river to drown himself? My husband and two other men saw him going into the water and restrained him. They persuaded him not to do it. He is the only child of his widowed mother, you know."

My informant paused before continuing. "I've been listening to what you have said to people this morning. If you're not afraid of leprosy, I'll not be either." Then she added, "I know several others who have the disease."

A few days later she came and hesitantly pointed to a spot on the calf of her leg. "Is this leprosy?" she asked, hardly daring to speak the word. I examined the spot, relieved to find only another common skin condition. She rejoiced to be free of the secret dread she had carried.

We could only guess how many people in our region like Tube lived with dread, shame, and ever-increasing disfigurement and disability. ∎

ஒ20ை

Tip of an Iceberg

Needing advice concerning the treatment of Tube, my first leprosy patient, I invited Ruth Adams, the nurse he had gone to see, and Barbara Morgan, another OMF leprosy-trained nurse, to come for a visit.

When I asked Tube if he knew others with the disease who might like to meet the nurses, he responded immediately. "Oh, yes, many! Actually several have already asked about the medicine I am taking." He agreed to invite those he knew with symptoms to his home on a prearranged date.

In an effort to spread the word further, we asked two of our language teachers to tell their neighbors across the river of the nurses' proposed visit. One responded with shock. "Leprosy?" she said. "Why would you want to do leprosy work? There's no leprosy here!" After her initial outburst she added, "If you really want to help Thai people, why don't you do

something worthwhile, like starting a kindergarten?"
She had a four-year-old. Later she admitted that she
knew of one person who *might* have the disease and
agreed to let him know.

By mid-morning on the appointed day, several folk
stood at our door. We directed them to Tube's house.

It was past noon before Barbara and Ruth arrived.
Having traveled in open buses and trains since early
morning, they looked hot, tired, dusty, and ready for a
bath. In Thailand bathing two or three times a day is
common—so common, in fact, that "Have you had
your bath yet?" is as natural a greeting to them as
"Hello, how are you?" is to us.

After the two nurses had bathed and eaten, we
went to Tube's house. Twelve pairs of anxious eyes
followed our progress up the bamboo ladder into the
house. Tube's mother received us graciously. Spread-
ing the guest mat on the floor, she brought us each a
glass of water. "It's safe," she assured us. "It's pure
rain water." Looking around the group, I recognized
the young man I had seen earlier trying to hide
behind the post of the granary.

The nurses took histories, examined each person,
then charted their findings. All twelve, including a
five-year-old, had reached advanced stages of leprosy.
Emotional pain had etched its mark on every face.

Though it was late when Barbara and Ruth finished, no one moved to leave. The patients listened
intently, and so did I, as the nurses outlined the
schedule of medicines and method of treatment. "We
cannot guarantee a cure for your disease," the nurses

explained, "but this medicine will check its progress. We will teach you how to care for your hands and feet to prevent further deformities." Hope rose visibly. The nurses continued: "This medicine is very potent. It cannot be given without supervision." Heads nodded, and eyes turned knowingly to Tube. "At first you will need to come to one of our clinics every week."

Faces clouded. "Oh, but we can't do that!" the leprosy sufferers exclaimed. "They won't let some of us on boats, buses, or the train. You must come here."

Already committed to an expanding work in their own district, my friends shook their heads. A silence, heavy with desperate disappointment, followed.

Then Tube spoke: "Why can't Miss Mary supervise our treatment? She's a nurse."

The suggestion dismayed me. I knew very little about leprosy, even less about its treatment. In fact, that afternoon had been my first real introduction to the complex disease. Yet how could I refuse after all I had seen and heard in the previous few hours? Each one gathered in Tube's house had a similar story. All had suffered through one "guaranteed cure" after another and spent hundreds of *baht*, only to watch their bodies become more and more painfully afflicted and misshapen.

Barbara and Ruth turned to me. "Could you? Would you?" they asked. "We could possibly come every two or three months to check on these folks if you would supervise their weekly care."

I bombarded Heaven with an urgent, silent prayer. "All right," I whispered after the hesitation. "With

God's help, I'll do what I can."

It was dark as we prepared to leave. "Mary will meet you here next week at ten in the morning," one of the nurses announced. "We will not be here. We have to leave tomorrow morning for another clinic."

Again an outcry. "Oh, please, please stay just one more day. We know many too shy to come today."

Chuen, the young man I had seen earlier, pleaded, "You *must* come to my house before you go. Please! I live just across the river near the ferry landing. In the morning I will meet you there and take you to them. I know they will want your medicine. You can still be in time for the train."

Our friends agreed.

We had barely reached home that evening when a man in government uniform climbed our steps. He had hesitated to go to Tube's house because he knew he would lose his position if his leprosy became known.

Shortly after sunup the next morning another four people waited at our door. Ruth Adams examined them briefly and advised them to return the following week. We then set off for our appointment. Ruthie Metcalf, my housemate, and Barbara had gone on ahead. As Ruth Adams and I hurried along the path to town, our neighbors called, "Where are you going so early?"

"To the ferry," we answered.

"It's hot walking. Why don't you take a boat from here?" they suggested.

So, settling on the fare with the owner of a small boat tethered nearby, we followed him down to the river's edge. Ruth turned to me and remarked, "See that light patch on his ankle? That's leprosy."

We climbed into the boat. "Where are you going so early?" he inquired as he pushed out into the current.

"We promised to meet some folk with a skin disease, who live on the other side of the river."

"I have leprosy," the man volunteered.

"Yes, I know. I saw," my companion said.

The boatman flinched, missed a stroke with his oar, and remained silent. "Would you like medicine for your disease?" Ruth asked.

His earnest "Yes!" sounded to me like a drowning man grasping for a floating log. Before leaving home that morning, we had asked God to lead us to those who needed us. He had begun answering already!

We made the crossing and found the other two waiting for us at the tea shop near the ferry landing. "Chuen has not come," they said, "but look at this crowd!" The curious had gathered, wondering why the foreigners had come and what they had to sell.

"We have medicine for leprosy," we told them, and our reply was relayed to the edge of the crowd. An older woman shepherding two small boys pushed through the group. Experienced eyes told our friends that the older child certainly had the disease, but probably not the younger one. Grunts from the assembled company indicated general agreement.

Next a teen-age girl with a deep scar on her fore-
arm stepped forward. She had once endured a common treatment for leprosy, the burning of the suspected area with chemicals or a hot iron. The visiting
nurses didn't think the girl had the disease, but advised her to come back in six months.

Some asked the price of the medicine. When the
nurses explained that this medicine could not be sold
or taken without a thorough examination and regular
supervision, many drifted away.

Chuen still had not come. We decided that two of
us would take the path upriver, the other two downriver, to see if we could find him. We would return
and meet before train time.

Ruth Adams and I turned northward. People stood
at gates or in doorways watching as we passed. They
neither spoke nor responded to our greetings. How
different from the times we'd come with books to sell!

After a time it seemed advisable to return to the
wharf. As Ruth and I turned to retrace our steps, those
who'd been staring after us stood as if glued to the
spot, like a motion picture abruptly stopped. Fearful,
hostile eyes fastened on us. Fear nibbled at my heart.
Some watchers backed away; others, apparently encouraged by sheer numbers, stood their ground,
silently scrutinizing us.

*F*inally an obviously appointed spokesman asked,
"How expensive is your medicine?"

"About fifteen cents a month," we answered, turning to move on.

"Wait!" the man called.

People looked from one to another. The spokesman nodded. Mechanically a young woman moved forward. "What is this?" she asked, nervously pointing to her shoulder. My friend examined the light patch on the girl's skin. She did not think it was leprosy, but asked if she might do a simple test. To demonstrate the procedure, she blindfolded me and, lightly brushing places on my exposed skin with a tiny piece of soft paper, asked me to point to each place I felt the touch of the paper. When the demonstration ended, I removed the blindfold.

"This is the way we look for numb areas," Ruth explained. "There's always numbness with leprosy."

Giggling nervously, the young woman consented to the examination. The curious pressed closer. The examinee pointed to every spot the paper touched. She had no numb areas. Relieved, the girl jerked the blindfold from her eyes and beamed broadly. She had passed the test! The crowd sighed their relief.

"Come along!" the spokesman called sharply.

We hurried after the retreating man, and a silent crowd followed. To myself I thought, *We must look like the entourage of the Pied Piper of Hamlin!*

The resolute spokesman finally stopped before a small dressmaker's shop. Bounding over vegetables laid out to dry on the steps, he spoke hastily to someone inside. Those who trailed pressed closer to hear the conversation. Shortly a girl of about ten emerged from the back of the shop. The man thrust her forward with the words, "Here! She has it."

It was obvious. Even I could see that the child had leprosy. Ruth examined her gently as she had done with the other young woman only moments before. This examination, however, revealed large areas where the child felt no touch of the paper. When the blindfold was removed from the eyes of the trembling waif, the man pushed her. "Go call your mother!" he commanded

The child retreated, protesting, "She won't come."

Nor did she. The child returned alone. With threats, the man again commanded her to get her mother. This time she refused.

From the muttering around us, we gathered that the mother also had the disease.

"Why don't *you* go to see *her*?" someone suggested.

"We will if you will show us the way," we said.

A buxom woman from the shop volunteered. We followed her down the narrow lane beside her shop. This time the curious did not follow. High bamboo fences bordered the lane. In the distance we heard wrangling voices. Finally our escort stopped. "Go on!" she said, giving us a gentle shove before retreating.

The little girl we had just examined raced past. Then we saw Chuen, who motioned for us to come ahead. Quickening our pace, we followed him into the courtyard toward a sputtering, hostile woman.

Not yet middle-aged, she sat on a wide bamboo bench under a large teakwood house on stilts. With stubbed fingers she clutched a tiny baby to her breast. Her face was swollen and lumpy, her ear lobes enlarged and thick. "Go away!" she cried. "We don't want your medicine. We're too poor. Get out!"

Chuen went to her side. "Older Sister," he said, "their medicine isn't expensive, and it's good. It is only five cents a week and will cost us just fifteen cents a month because every fourth week we don't need to take it."

The woman grew less aggressive. Turning inflamed eyes toward us, she said, "We've tried many kinds of medicine and all sorts of treatment. Now look at us! We're no better. No, there's nothing now for us but to die. Maybe the next life around will be better. I don't want to try anything more."

Chuen laid his hand on his sister's shoulder. "Sister Hieng, listen! Please listen to what the foreign doctor is saying." (In those days anyone who treated sickness was called "doctor.")

As Ruth carefully outlined the course of treatment, the woman's attitude softened further. "All right," the sick mother said wearily, only barely convinced, "we'll try your medicine for a while."

"For a person who has had the disease as long as you have," Ruth countered, "you will probably need the medicine the rest of your life. But you will feel stronger and have relief from your pain and further crippling. Your baby will be protected too."

We waited while the woman considered her options. Then, quite without warning, she shouted, "Chaub! Come here!"

From a nearby house another family member came reluctantly down the steps. He, too, was badly disfigured. As the three siblings talked together, I understood why they had been unwilling to face the mob on the street.

At last the household of sufferers agreed to treatment. As we examined them, we learned that their mother, once a wealthy woman, had also suffered the ravages of leprosy. Another sister, the seamstress in the shop we had stopped at, did not have the disease.

Listening to their heart-breaking story, I wondered how many generations had passed on this dreadful disease and how many more might suffer if it remained unchecked.

Train time neared. Our friends had to leave. "I'll come again next week," I told the family.

We returned to the lane with the high barriers, obviously erected in an effort to isolate the disease.

Suddenly the enormity of the task to which I had consented rolled over me. Everywhere I saw the compelling need for individual health care and public health education. In just twenty-four hours we had discovered nineteen leprosy sufferers.

The words of our language teacher buzzed in my mind: "Why should you want to do leprosy work? There's no leprosy here!" The one who uttered those words lived only five or six houses from the pathetic family we had just visited.

I had glimpsed only the tip of an iceberg. ■

❧21☙
Coming to Grips
with a Monster

Little did I imagine the dimensions of the monstrous iceberg of leprosy that lurked below the surface. For centuries Hindu and Buddhist philosophers had considered suffering to be the natural consequence of evil done in a former incarnation. That belief tended to erase compassion. It reinforced the idea that nothing could or should be done to alleviate misery. Most people stoically accepted suffering as deserved.

After that initial visit by Barbara North and Ruth Adams, people who had or feared they had the disease besieged us. Some begged me to visit a family member or a friend too sick or crippled to come to our house.

I found leprosy sufferers in appalling conditions. Families secreted them away in hot, dark rooms. One lived in a dingy corner of a cargo boat. Others lived alone in miserable shacks. Often rats nibbled at numb feet and hands while the victims slept.

Calls for help came from farther and farther afield. Locating and visiting them took hours, sometimes whole days. Every plea I responded to heightened my sense of need for training. So when another nurse could come to relieve me, I gratefully attended a special training course taught by Leprologists Paul Brand and Richard Buker, veterans of years of service and experience in India and Thailand.

Returning from those intense weeks, I knew I had to make changes. To continue making fifty or sixty home visits every week was irrational. In addition, an increasing flood of people came to our home for examination and treatment, something neither advisable nor appropriate. We had to find a more suitable place away from thickly populated riverbank areas, yet accessible for those with crippled or ulcerated feet.

We found a place near the rice mill not far from Chuen's home. Patients could reach it by following ox-cart tracks across fields or by taking a freight lane that led up from the river to the mill.

Chuen negotiated the rental of a tiny plot of land hidden from the mill by huge piles of rice husks. There we built an open-sided, bamboo-and-thatch shelter. A four-by-six-foot table provided a place for patients to sit while having dressings done and three long stationary benches made space for those waiting.

Many patients balked when I told them I could no

longer come to their homes, that they must now go to the new central clinic. "But I've not gone anywhere in years! I'm too sick to go so far," they declared. "Maybe others are able, but I'm not. You must come to me!"

I felt torn. I understood their pleas but knew my own limitations—and I had to be consistent. If I went to one, I had to go to all. That became impossible as the numbers grew. It grieved me to see severely afflicted patients go off medication; yet eventually most came to the new clinic.

Tube became an able assistant. A patient himself, he understood our routines, medicines, and treatments and could explain them in a way that eased patients' fears and concerns. He kept patient charts and accounts while I examined new patients, dispensed medicines, and did dressings.

Fellow missionaries came with me on clinic days to chat with the people waiting. Scripture posters and well-thumbed picture rolls on the life of Jesus invariably drew questions. The painting of the crucifixion of Jesus particularly opened opportunities to tell what He has done for us. Before long Tube was also telling the story.

As I scraped deep, crusted ulcers on feet that felt no pain, I often heard people say, "Ah, she's making a lot of merit doing that." In Thai culture, feet are considered to be the most ignoble part of the body; to touch them or be touched by them is degrading.

"But I'm not doing this to gain merit," I told them. "God's Son, Jesus Christ, has already made merit for us. Jesus did all that was ever needed to be done to take away our sin by dying in our place. We came to Thailand not only to bring healing, but to tell you about Him so that you may know and love Him too." Over the months we watched comprehension dawn in minds long blinded by tradition. Among the first to accept Christ were Tube and Chuen.

When patients stabilized on the new medicine and learned how to exercise and how to protect their numb hands and feet, I could let them extend their times between visits. That eased the strain of travel for them and gave me opportunity to respond to other needs.

*I*f ten or more patients came from a certain locality, I considered starting a clinic there. From a man named Nan I learned about a pocket of severely infected people in a village about an hour and a half downriver. "My sister and I live in a house right on the river," Nan said, begging me to come. "You can come by boat and use our house as a place to treat people."

I agreed to go. The long-distance passenger boats stopped only at large cities, but small boats zigzagged across the river to pick up any who hailed them. Those boats usually left our city in the morning and returned in the evening.

On our first visit Nan and his sister Nee warmly welcomed fellow worker Gerry Stockley and me. Several people had gathered and eagerly awaited our examination. None were more severely crippled than our host and hostess. I wondered how, in their condition, they could keep a house so spotlessly clean, and remarked about their gleaming floor. With proud, partially paralyzed faces, the two smiled. "We wax it regularly," they told me, "with fresh coconut."

On our second visit to Nan and Nee's home, friends of a leprosy sufferer in a nearby house asked if we would go see her. "She isn't able to come here," they explained.

As we approached the house, I saw a girl, probably in her late teens, lying under the house. With a burlap rice bag as her only covering, she lay on a soiled, ragged mat spread over the bamboo trestle table that served as her bed. Flies crawled over purulent sores on every exposed surface of her body. The sight and smell was nauseating.

Praying for control, I went to her side. As I touched her hand, she struggled to sit up. Turning blind eyes toward me, she asked, pleading, "Will your medicine cure me?"

"No, dear," I had to tell her honestly, "but it will dry and help heal these sores and make you stronger to fight the disease."

I cleaned and dressed as many of the ulcers as I was able with the solutions and dressings I had brought with me. Gerry told her about Jesus. The girl listened intently. Tears welled in her puffy eyes. I gave her family medicines, told them how to give them, and promised to return the following week.

As we turned to leave, those who had gathered to watch and listen pushed first one person and another toward us to be examined. I found six of them in various stages of leprosy.

Returning to Nan's house, I was thankful to be away from the dreadful stench, but more grateful for the opportunity to share Jesus' love.

Coming to Grips with a Monster

As we waited for the evening boat, Nan said, "Next time come on the earliest boat. The ice boat returns around ten. I have a friend who gets ice each day, and he'll tell the pilot to stop for you. That will let you get home before noon."

The next week we caught the six a.m. boat. Patients already awaited us. "It won't take you long today," they said. "Remember the girl you went to see last week? She died yesterday."

I was shocked—but so grateful we'd had the opportunity to show our love and tell her about God's greater love.

*L*ater that morning, as I did Nee's dressings, she said, "You know, I've thought about what you said about Jesus and His dying on the cross. I've always wondered if giving food to the priests would insure a better life for us in our next incarnation. How can we know when we've made enough merit?"

We talked as I worked. I had barely finished when someone shouted, "Here comes the ice boat!"

In spite of loud shouting and wild hand-waving, the boat chugged on past. The pilot did not look our way once! My heart sank. We could expect no other boats until evening.

With the pressure now off, we had time to enjoy our friendly, chatty patients. In the ease of conversation we almost forgot we were foreigners.

By eleven we had seen most patients. Because we had expected to be home for lunch, we had brought no food. At someone's suggestion we walked into the village and found a noodle shop. While enjoying a hot meal, we noticed a stall next door selling hand-woven straw mats. We bought two, thinking we could nap on them while waiting for the evening boat.

We postponed our naps when the young patient who had accompanied us to the village invited us to his house. "Please come for a little while. It isn't far. It's right on the riverbank, so if a boat comes, we can hail it from there."

The news of our coming preceded us. After the initial flurry of welcome, we discovered that several in the large group waiting for us wanted us to check them for leprosy. A sister of our escort plainly had the disease. She was one who earlier had not braved leaving her home.

When we returned to Nan and Nee's, they asked, "Where have you been for so long?" They nodded knowingly when we told them. They already knew!

Nee admired our new mats, spread them on the floor, and invited us to sit down for a chat. She, her brother, and the young man from whose home we had just come, turned the conversation immediately to Jesus. They were full of questions.

Gerry took out her English Bible and gave a Thai New Testament to the younger man, the only one able to read. We responded to their questions by finding suitable answers in our English Bible, then helping the young reader find the same text in Thai. The three were excited by each new truth. When we came to

Coming to Grips with a Monster

Jesus' words, "Feed my sheep," addressed to Peter in John 21:17 (KJV), Nee asked, "Who are the sheep?"

With stubby hands partially-sighted Nan thumped his chest, exclaiming, "Me! Us!"

Reading on, we came to Jesus' post-resurrection encounter with Thomas. The young man read aloud: "Because you have seen me, Thomas, you have believed. Blessed are they that have not seen, and yet have believed" (John 20:29, KJV).

"Who do you think those people are?" I asked.

The reader, absorbed in the narrative, seemed impatient at the interruption. But with a tolerant smile and sweep of his hand, he answered, "Why, that's us, all of us here, isn't it?"

For nearly two hours we searched and read Scripture after Scripture. "Yes! Yes! Now I understand," Nan exclaimed. "If I confess my sin to this Jesus and tell Him I believe He took it all away when He died on the cross, I will become God's child. Right? Is this how to ask?" Immediately he began the most natural and childlike prayer I have ever heard. "Was that right? Am I now God's child?" he asked earnestly when finished.

I blinked back tears as I assured him that he was.

"With this disease," Nan continued thoughtfully, "they won't let us be cremated at the temple. They just put us in the ground. But that doesn't matter now, does it? My spirit will already be safe with Jesus, and I won't have to come back and be incarnated again and again, will I?" The radiance of his face wonderfully confirmed his acceptance into God's family.

We had scarcely noticed the fierce afternoon sun beating on the tin roof until Nee announced, "Time to take a rest!"

She shooed the men down the steps with instructions to go for Coca Cola. From her room she brought two pillows and tossed them onto our new mats, inviting us to nap. Glancing at the oily pillows, we spread our handkerchiefs over them and lay down. We asked the Lord to take care of the rest!

Too excited to sleep, Gerry and I lay quietly for a while. Nee went to the edge of the verandah and, squatting down, told the neighbors about our conversation. Later she heard us whispering and came thumping across the floor on toeless feet and sat down beside us. "Let's talk some more about Jesus," she said.

Later the men returned with warm Cokes, which we drank, grateful for something wet. In no time, it seemed, the neighbors called, "Here comes the boat!"

On our upriver trip home we talked of all God had done that day. How perfect His timing had been! We missed the ice boat because He had special work for us to do. The evening boat came when we had completed His work. And we still reached home in time to share highlights of our eventful day with our evening English class. ∎

ಜ22ೞ

Unanticipated
Solution

As the numbers of leprosy patients increased, so did occasions for concern. Two things I feared: a renewed invasion of leprosy in a body already weakened by the disease and injury to hands, feet, or eyes insensitive to pain. I yearned for closer professional supervision, and I needed somewhere to refer bad cases. The few hospitals that existed at the time did not accept patients with leprosy. Daily, as I responded to pressing needs, I prayed for wisdom in treatment, protection from error, and stamina to continue.

One day sympathetic neighbors bringing a very sick lad told a tale of frustration in trying to get the boy to the clinic. A compassionate bus driver finally yielded to their pleas to let them aboard with, "All right, but just this once!"

"Couldn't you begin a clinic in our province?" they

pled. "We will find a place if you will come." My answer had to be yes.

The first site suggested, a rural, wayside bus stop near the child's home, was far too public. Further search brought to light a much more suitable site atop a section of Lopburi's old city wall. With official permission to use a quiet corner on the time-worn bulwark, we moved ahead. The unpretentious little shelter cost only twenty-one dollars U.S. and blended harmoniously into the ancient bastion. Even squeals and grunts from pigs in a pen just beyond a patch of sweet corn did not diminish my joy the day we held our first clinic there.

But the absence of the child who had prompted this new outreach disturbed me. "He's too ill to come today," volunteered one of his neighbors. "His mother says it's too far for him to come here. Besides, he has to tend the water buffalo."

Sensing my disappointment, the informant offered to take the boy's medicine to him. "I'm sorry, but I can't give you his medicine," I said. "I'll need to see him first; I'll stop by on my way home this afternoon."

Many new patients came that day, among them a man who had been drinking, probably to bolster his courage. To clean and dress his many ulcers took more than two hours. As I worked, I wondered if the time and effort was worthwhile. To my co-worker I even remarked, "These dressings will probably all be off by the time he staggers home."

Thirty years later I revisited that now enlarged

clinic and met the man again. When introduced, he reminded me of that first day and the thirty-three dressings I did for him. Though deformities remain, his leprosy is healed. What's more, he is a new man, both inside and out—a leader of the local group of believers. Those two hours of work worthwhile? Infinitely!

Another new patient that day was a woman whose husband had cast her away following the birth of their first child, when he discovered she had leprosy. Like tuberculosis, leprosy may lie dormant in a strong body for years, manifesting itself only after injury, illness, or a debilitating delivery, as in Sai's case. Sai came regularly for treatment and eventually became a valued helper at the clinic.

On my way home that day I made a detour toward the farmhouse where the young absentee lived. The child, asleep, lay on the back of a water buffalo grazing in the sun. At his mother's call, he slid off the animal and limped painfully toward me. His pinched face and sunken eyes told me how ill he was. I touched his parched and burning cheek.

At that, his mother hastened to assure me she had given him nothing to drink all day—a prohibition the Thai have practiced since olden days. I wanted to gather the child in my arms and run with him to a hospital, but I knew that no hospital would accept him. I could only instruct his mother to bathe him, another taboo, and give him liquids to drink I gave her medicine for his pain and fever.

Wearied and sick at heart, I turned to go, wondering if the mother would follow any of my instructions. I shall never know. The child died a few days later.

I returned to the road and climbed onto the next bus that halted before me in a cloud of dust. Sinking onto the wooden bench, I cried silently, *When, Lord, will we have a hospital where sufferers like this little fellow can be cared for?*

The answer to that prayer was surprisingly nearer than I imagined!

Returning home, I found a copy of OMF's in-house publication in the mail. Thumbing through it, I came upon an article outlining the mission's proposed medical program in central Thailand. *This should be interesting,* I thought as I sat on the steps to read. Scanning the article, my eyes fell on my name. It followed the designation **"Manorom Christian Hospital Matron."** I could not believe what I read!

True, I had volunteered to go to Thailand as a member of the medical team, and I had said I liked institutional nursing. But being a director of nursing services had never crossed my mind. Shock waves rolled over me. *Surely it's not true! It can't be,* my heart cried. *I'm not trained in administration, nor do I have enough Thai language to train a national staff. Besides, I'm not a leader!*

Indignation rose within me. Why hadn't I been asked or informed about this decision? I stumbled to my bedroom. Forgetting my usual precaution of first shedding contaminated clothing and bathing before going to my room, I flung myself on the bed. *How could this incredible situation have happened? Surely it was a mistake, a printing error!*

As I struggled with my thoughts, the Lord reminded me of the words of Naomi to her daughter-in-law, Ruth, when things looked uncertain: "Sit still, my daughter, until you know how the matter will fall" (Ruth 3:18, KJV). My eyes then caught the words of a motto hung on my wall: "Be still and know that I am God" (Ps. 46:10, KJV). The instruction to "Sit still" and "Be still" helped quiet my agitated heart.

How often I had wished for a place where patients with serious complications could receive care in ways not possible in our rudimentary clinics! Even earlier in the day I had been desperate for such a haven for the boy baking without water on the back of the water buffalo. Could it be in God's great plan that I should have a part in a hospital that would accept leprosy patients along with others in need? The possibilities awed me.

Several weeks after I read that disquieting article, the official letter of appointment came. Though it brought renewed perplexity, I breathed a prayer of thanks for the time I'd had to consider the appointment before I needed to reply.

Not long afterwards Dr. Chris Maddox, Medical Superintendent for our central Thailand field, came to discuss details of starting the small rural hospital. Accompanying him was Edith Schlatter, one of the nurses with whom I would work. As we exchanged ideas, I began to realize how diverse the practices and expectations of our multi-national team would be. The envisioned team would come from Australia, England, New Zealand, Switzerland, Thailand, and U.S.A. We would need God's enabling grace to function together in harmony.

I first visited the hospital site near the small market town of Manorom to attend a conference for leprosy workers. For a change of pace one evening several of us walked from the mission house in town to the construction site, about a quarter of a mile away. As we drew near, I gazed at skeletal structures rising in a rice field just beyond the narrow, rutted lane on which we approached.

On a hastily arranged tour of the site, Dr. Maddox led the way. We stepped carefully around scaffolding and framework in the unfinished structures. "This will be a consulting room; here, the business office; there, the pharmacy, and that will be the lab," he said. He guided us on to the operating and X-ray rooms. Pointing down the corridor, he added, "That is where the delivery room, nursery, and wards will be."

As we moved from place to place, Dr. Maddox talked enthusiastically about things he had ordered from overseas—electric generator, X-ray machine, operating table, sterilizers, beds, diagnostic equipment, and surgical instruments.

In place of the piles of earth, bags of cement, and stacks of lumber, our guide envisioned the little hospital already set up and humming efficiently to meet the needs of the sick. By contrast, I thought about details: What about medicine and dressing trays, surgical drapes and gowns, pillows and mattresses? Where would they come from? We would need laundry and cleaning equipment. What about national staff? Who would train them into strange new jobs and instruct them in the use of unfamiliar equipment?

Perplexed and overwhelmed by the enormity of the task that lay ahead, I wanted to run back to the conference and beg to remain on the leprosy team. I could not. Hadn't I promised to serve wherever I could fill a need? Here it was!

On the way back to the village with the others, I prayed passionately, *O God, how I need Your help! I need Your wisdom for this incredible job. Help me lay hold of it by trusting only in You! I cannot do it any other way.* I would have truly panicked had I known I wouldn't return until just four weeks before the opening. In infinite love, God shielded me from that knowledge.

My work at the clinics continued unabated after the leprosy conference. At the same time our home hummed with added activity. Dr. Maddox had asked me to prepare a list of simple necessities that could be purchased locally for the new hospital.

Unsure of what all "simple" included, I began my list at the bottom with safety pins, paper clips, and writing materials. To these I added tiny Chinese wine cups for dispensing medicines, small enamel rice basins, and handleless tea cups for solutions on dressing trays. We would need hand fans for feverish patients and spittoons for beetle-nut-chewing ones. Tiny kerosene lamps for each bedside could serve well as night lights when the electric generator was turned off at ten. We would need anti-ant pots in which to set the legs of baby cots to keep stinging ants from crawling up to the newborn. As I tried to envision other needs, I added mosquito netting, flannelette, unbleached muslin, toweling, canvas, and plastic sheeting. When the lists were approved, shopping began.

Our house took on the appearance of a general and yard-goods store. I engaged neighbors with sewing machines to convert bales of netting and bolts of muslin into bed- and cot-sized nets and sheets. From other bolts of muslin, I cut multi-sized surgical gowns, drapes, and double-thickness wrappers for bundling equipment to be sterilized. Yards of plastic and canvas became mattress covers. Rolls of soft toweling, cut and hemmed, made satisfactory wash cloths and baby diapers. To help the laundress later get linens back to the appropriate departments, we color-coded each piece—red for outpatients, green for surgery, blue for wards, and so on.

Living space in our little house diminished drastically as purchases mounted and sewing helpers returned the finished items. Now and again, the doctor came to report on building progress and took away some accumulated stock, temporarily giving us space in which to move about and breathe!

Ruth Adams, the nurse appointed to take over my leprosy work, came to live with us. Every night after she moved into my room I made up my bed on our dining table. Week by week we visited the various clinics to introduce her to the patients.

*F*inally the day came for me to leave Singburi, my first Thailand home. Amid assorted suitcases and a trunk of personal things, jumbled boxes and bags of hospital supplies, the hospital vehicle hustled me off to my new home.

Sadness washed over me as we drove past familiar paths along the way. I had walked many of them on my way to find new patients or to take medicine to someone too ill to come to the clinic. I had learned to care about each of my patients and would miss them. But I knew someone would be taking care of them, and I rejoiced that during my time with them many had improved physically and, most wonderfully, some had chosen to follow the Savior. ■

ಐ23ಲ
A Hospital from Scratch

We arrived at Manorom toward evening. How different it looked! Now a graded lane led from the highway to the nearly completed hospital buildings. Staff houses, the kitchen, laundry and generator sheds all blended harmoniously with the surrounding paddy fields of ripening rice. How peaceful the scene looked at dusk!

In the days that followed, however, peace gave way to frantic activity as we raced toward opening day less than a month away. My stress level rose to dizzying heights.

The morning after my arrival Dr. Maddox asked me to come for "a look around." I soon realized the utter inadequacy of my list of "simple things." I had not imagined that a chart rack, medicine cabinets, storage and linen cupboards, bedside lockers, and baby cots fit into the "simple" category. These now had to be designed and carpenters found to make them.

We urgently needed to select and begin training
teenage Thai girls as aides in the hospital. But teaching
could not begin until all missionary nurses agreed on
the methods we would all use. I could not have
imagined how many "right," but totally different ways
we discovered for doing even the simplest procedure!

Interviewing, selecting, and teaching Thai women
and men to be hospital cleaners, laundresses, and
gardeners also demanded wisdom and tact. We
needed staff to help in our homes too. I would have
preferred to do household tasks myself, but working
in the hospital nine to thirteen hours a day made that
impossible. Shopping daily at the outdoor market for
fresh food, preparing meals, and doing personal laundry without modern equipment would take more
hours than we had. Introducing new househelpers to
breadmaking and the preparation of at least some
meals without rice took both patience and a sense of
humor—and sometimes a strong stomach!

The intense activity at the hospital accelerated as
opening day drew near. Carpenters, electricians,
painters, plumbers, and workmen sanding floors—all
unused to deadlines—tumbled over one another to
complete their work. As invitations had already gone
out to government officials and others, we could not
postpone the opening.

Equipment ordered from overseas had been held
up at customs in Bangkok for many days. Without it,
we wouldn't look much like a hospital! The equipment
cleared customs *one day* before opening. On the way to

Bangkok the truck hired to collect the shipment broke down. We engaged another. Throughout that unforgettable night, I awakened to every sound, wondering, *Is that our truck?*

Saturday, August 18, 1956, dawned overcast and cool. Grateful for the break from the heat, we hustled to complete preparations. By noon we were as ready as possible. Fellow missionaries and a few guests had already arrived for the four p.m. ceremony. We had gone to lunch when a shout echoed across the compound: "Here comes the truck!"

Literally everyone ran outside. The heavily laden vehicle pulled to a stop beside the hospital. Doffing his cap, the driver beamed. He had made it!

Willing hands and strong arms hastily unloaded heavy crates and cartons. Frantically helpers pried them open, unwrapped and identified the contents, and whisked items to their assigned places.

When crews delivered beds to the wards, they discovered that only two had springs. The bare frames of the rest could not be made up with bedding. Surveying the pile of wrappings, cardboard, and cord that littered the ward floor, someone suggested: "Let's tie these bits of cord together and weave them back and forth across the metal frames. We can lay the larger pieces of cardboard on top of the cord as temporary bedboards to support the mattresses."

In minutes eighteen tidy and sturdy looking beds lined the wards. As we finished the task, someone said, "As long as no one tries them out, all should be well."

By three o'clock the crew had carried the last bits of trash away, and we scampered off to dress in uniform.

In our rush to set up and place the delayed equipment, most of us had not noticed the brooding skies. Minutes before the ceremony was to begin, torrents of rain lashed the buildings and sent the assembled guests crowding into the hospital for shelter. Our Thai guests nodded and smiled as they watched the downpour. "M-m-m," they murmured, "a good omen! The heavens are pouring their blessing on our new hospital!"

I was not inclined to agree with our exuberant guests as I looked at recently vacated chairs awash in sand and clay at the front of the hospital. I watched with horror as the furious gale tore down decorations and toppled the outdoor screen put up for an evening film showing. Inwardly I sighed, knowing that feet now sloshing through swirling waters would soon be grinding gravel and mud into our spotless floors!

The squall subsided. With eyes on the clouds, participants shortened their speeches and prayers. The sodden veil over the hospital's nameplate was drawn aside. We were declared "Open."

New employees now scattered to assigned posts where they would open doors to receive guests. I followed to check each department before the onslaught of visitors.

At the door of one ward a distraught aide met me in tears. "Look," she cried, pointing to a bed. Bedding, mattress and cardboard lay in a rumpled heap on the floor. Dangling bits of cord hung from the frame. "A naughty boy just came in and tried to lie on it," she complained.

Hurrying to the jumbled mess, we retied the ruptured cords and repositioned the cardboard and mattress. We must have broken all speed records for bedmaking. We had barely finished when Dr. Maddox ushered the Provincial Governor and his party into the ward!

Thunder continued to rumble, so local villagers did not linger. Visiting missionaries and their friends kindly lent a hand with clean-up. They wiped down tables and chairs, mopped floors, and helped prepare an evening communal meal. Others dismantled the makeshift beds and made up mattresses on the floor for stranded guests. In the larger ward other helpers set up chairs and the movie projector for an indoor showing of a film later in the evening.

Well past midnight I went to my room. Wrung out, but too tired to sleep, I lay thinking over the turmoil and confusion of the day and weeks just past. For most of that pell-mell day my thanksgiving key had lain unused, except for the moment the truck arrived. Despite our mistakes, God had graciously enabled us to put together from scratch the Manorom Christian Hospital, no mean accomplishment.

*E*arly the next morning staff, visitors, and a large crowd of villagers gathered beside a pond to witness Manorom's first baptisms. Five men made public their confession of Christ. For the little group of Christians present, it was a joyful hour.

In the weeks that followed, we saw many "firsts." The staff saw their first patient, their first operation, their first delivery. They also saw their first hemorrhage and death. Working beside missionary personnel, new trainees learned to care for those suffering from beri-beri, anemia, pneumonia, malaria, typhoid, tuberculosis, and leprosy. They assisted with the treatment of nasty burns, shattering road injuries, and knife and gunshot wounds.

It was an abrupt and headlong leap for the national staff into the strange world of Western medicine. Most of the youthful, rural staff had only an elementary education and still believed all sorts of old wives' tales. Some responded with amazing adaptability, becoming able, long-term assistants.

For others the plunge was too great. These simply failed to report for duty. We regretted losing them, but rejoiced for the brief opportunity we'd had to touch their lives for Christ.

When time came for my home leave six months after the hospital's opening, I felt more than ready for rest, change, and further training. ■

⊷24℃

Under His Wings

During my second furlough—now known as "home assignment"—sharing with family and prayer partners came much more easily than it had been during the months after leaving China. This time I could speak freely of my work. Without hesitation I asked specific prayer for the duties and responsibilities I expected to resume at Manorom Christian Hospital.

The last week of my home assignment my family planned a reunion and a farewell for me. My sister Ruth brought mail for me that had accumulated at her home. Thirsty for news from the field, I tore open the letters from Thailand and read eagerly. Excitement turned to dismay. "You will not be returning to the hospital," I read. "You are to rejoin the leprosy team." The news—without a hint of explanation for the change of direction—stunned me, throwing me headlong into depression.

Because my Thai re-entry permit expired in eight days and all travel arrangements had been booked, I had to return to Thailand without delay, no matter how dispirited I felt. The turmoil in my heart and the turbulent weather our plane encountered made that trans-Pacific flight a long, lonely one.

In Singburi team members, old neighbors, and former patients welcomed me with genuine warmth. I knew the need and potential for leprosy work were as great as ever. Even so, the sense that I had failed at the hospital tormented me and robbed me of joy.

Finally the stern words of a wise counselor helped me see to the root of the problem. I was wallowing in self-pity, not because of where I served but because of pride. Once I dealt with my pride, my rusty "thanks-giving key" became operative again. Peace returned, tears dried—and I became easier to live with! With that settled, I plunged happily into leprosy work once again.

After finding shelter for my own buffeted spirit, I watched God shelter others.

A few months after returning to Singburi I escorted several leprosy patients to a conference planned especially for them. Like most Thai men and women of the time, we all wore the common ankle-length wrap-around skirt. In spite of tropical heat, most of my traveling companions also wore long-sleeved shirts or blouses for the three-hour journey in an effort to conceal telltale deformities. They covered crippled hands with extended cuffs or soft towels while I negotiated fares and tickets for them. Though their disease no longer posed a danger to others, they knew to expect rejection and cursing if suspected of having leprosy. I could not know the fears that lurked in their hearts as they left their homes that morning.

When I first saw the rustic conference facilities, I thought them totally inadequate. But conferees quickly made themselves at home in the country clinic and settled in to enjoy the days ahead.

The thatched roof of the old clinic had been extended to provide added seating and shelter from rain or sun. Floor boards and trestles loaned by a neighbor served as benches by day and, pushed together, beds by night.

A crude, lockable hut had been built to secure cooking utensils and food supplies. The "stove" was a series of small firepits dug into the hard, dry clay dike that ran along one side of the nearby paddy field. Over these firepits, large rice pots, kettles, and woks fitted perfectly. Busy attendants fed the necessary wood and charcoal through small openings at the side to produce high, medium, or low heat.

Other conferees carried water for food preparation and wash-up from a distant well, keeping the two fifty-gallon jars near the cook fires filled.

Under a clump of bamboo at the rear of the clinic jars of water and a dozen or so gourd dippers provided "showers." A temporary enclosure near the bath site served as a dressing area for the women. More private needs could be met out beyond the tall brush-covered ant hills that dotted surrounding rice fields.

In this simple setting those who came "to see Jesus" mingled together supportively and contentedly—and stole my heart.

The Lord spoke through the simple yet profound messages of an experienced Thai pastor. He emphasized the complete salvation we have in Jesus Christ and our obligation to live holy lives before God and our fellow man.

The last day of the conference inclement weather threatened. By afternoon a gusty wind kicked up dust and tore loose two sheets of thatch from the roof. Deft hands secured the flapping thatch to the supporting side posts of the shelter. "Great," someone exclaimed, "now we have two walls to keep the wind out!"

The pastor had resumed his message when a third piece of the roof blew loose. We sang while men repaired the damage. Another shout, "*Now* we have three side walls!" brought hilarious laughter. The pastor finished his message to a still-attentive audience as flashing lightning and cracking thunder warned of more storm on the way.

Three of the foreigners sped off on bikes to bring plastic sheeting and blankets from the mission house in town. Following quickly on foot, those of us staying in town had barely reached the house when the storm broke. Throughout the night, as the elements raged, we felt grave concern for our friends at the conference site. Would the loosely constructed shelter withstand such a furious wind-whipped downpour?

At dawn we picked our way around puddles of standing water and storm-downed debris, wondering what we might find.

Sai, my Lopburi clinic helper, seeing us from a distance, raced to meet us with joyous testimony. "Look!" she cried, "see what God did last night! Right after you left the whole shelter shook and rattled violently, but no more pieces of roof came off. We prayed, and—do you know what?—just when we thought the wind would blow the shelter away, the wind changed direction and died down. We were safe and sound in our three-sided house! Isn't God good!"

Looking at the dry ground around our feet, I asked, "But didn't it rain here at all last night?"

Others now gathered around us. "No!" they said, "It only sprinkled a little, just enough to settle dust and cool the air. Look, our firewood isn't even wet! Come, breakfast is ready—eat with us!"

Curious townspeople came along the still muddy road to see for themselves the only dry spot in the area. Some lingered safely behind the temporary walls and listened to the closing message. They had seen how God protected the people there. Now they heard the pastor explain that God's power is just as mighty to save and keep from sin those who trust in Him.

Just as we had prayed, the conference had been a time of shelter "under God's wings" for all who had come. As the retreat came to a close, the conferees seemed reluctant to leave.

Some weeks later I saw God extend His sheltering wings through a very different kind of storm. As I prepared for an evening English Bible class, I saw a

middle-aged couple coming down our lane. Their sad
faces prepared me for a request for me to visit someone sick or to examine one or both of them for leprosy.
With a sigh, I pushed my books aside and went to
meet them. Inviting them up to the verandah, I went
for cool drinking water. When I returned, the woman
spoke: "There is something troubling us. We have
been told you can help."

"Yes?" I said, sitting down beside her, fully expecting a tale of leprosy.

Instead she said, "I've had a dream about a man
called Jesus. Can you tell us about Him? We don't
really know much about Him except once we heard
His name."

Suddenly I was alert. The woman looked earnestly
into my eyes. "We've been seeking peace for many
years," she continued. "We have tried to live good
lives, like the Buddha taught. I even became a
[Buddhist] nun and spent weeks meditating in a cave,
but enlightenment never came. Our neighbors say we
are mad for seeking so earnestly. Do you think we are
mad?"

"No, I don't think you are mad," I said.

I went to get my Thai Bible and prayed for wisdom.
Returning, I opened to Scriptures that explain who
Jesus Christ, God's Son, really is and how He came
into the world to deal with our sin. Then turning to
Psalm 103:12, I asked the man to read the verse.

Adjusting a pair of spectacles with a broken bow,
he took the book and read the words, "As far as the
east is from the west, so far has God removed our

transgressions from us." He read the words again, then paused. "It says here God removes our sin. Does that mean we don't need to do merit to balance out the evil we have already done?"

"Tell me," I probed, "what does 'remove' mean?"

Pausing before he replied, he said, "I guess it means 'take away,' doesn't it?"

"That's right," I said. "Now tell me, how far is east from west?"

The man looked up. Turning his head first to the east and then toward the setting sun, he responded thoughtfully, "I don't know. They are too far apart—in opposite directions."

"Right!" I encouraged, "and that is how far our sins are removed when we confess them to Jesus. He died to take them right away. They can never be brought back to us or against us again. They are removed—gone!—gone as far as the east is from the west."

The man removed the spectacles and handed them to his wife. "Read this," he urged, pressing the Bible into her hand. Taking the spectacles and holding them close to her eyes, the woman followed her husband's finger as he pointed to each word. I watched, thrilled to see that she, too, grasped the meaning of that wonderful promise.

The hour was growing late, and the pair needed to get to the river before the last ferry crossed. I gave them a New Testament and urged them to read it and come again.

A week passed before the two returned. This time they climbed the steps to our house smiling broadly.

Ignoring the usual Thai greeting, they stretched their arms full length toward the east and west and exclaimed, "Jesus has taken our sins this far away! We have peace!"

After that visit the couple came frequently to read the Scripture or ask questions. Later they began to visit, share, and pray with leprosy patients they met. Ahead of their generation, this couple were to pay a heavy price for continuing to befriend leprosy sufferers.

The couple built a little house and there welcomed friends with leprosy. After a few months the owner of the property refused to extend their lease. "I'd rather have pigs or horses on my land than people with leprosy and you Christians," he said.

With aching hearts the couple dismantled their home and moved it away. I visited them later in another city and found them still joyfully trusting God and sheltering under His wings. Blang, the husband, now a gardener in a public park, shared his faith with people strolling in the park. Duey, his wife, continued her itinerant hair-cutting business and talked about her Savior to customers wherever she set her basket of barbering equipment down.

I also saw God provide shelter for a popular teenager who came to our English class. After a few months of classes, we sensed the lad's interest went beyond English to the content of our textbook, the New Testament.

Dit's first inquiries were, "Did the God you speak of

create our world? How is it possible to know who did? The venerable abbot at the temple next to our school says no one can truly know how our universe began. He says it happened through a reliable power, but we can't know who or what that power is."

We could tell that Dit was thinking and discussing with others the things he heard in our class. He came with questions often asked by our Buddhist friends: "Was Jesus really God? If so, couldn't He have stopped those who killed Him? If He was good, why did He receive evil? Buddha taught, 'Do good; receive good. Do evil; receive evil.' Did the things in this Book actually happen, or are they just legends? Did Jesus really die? Maybe they just thought He died, then revived. Or perhaps they saw a spirit like people sometimes see today."

One day a very different question surprised and encouraged me. "If Jesus is God and He left Heaven to become like us and die in our place to take away the penalty for sins, then we don't have to keep on doing merit to pay for our sins, do we?"

"No, we don't," I agreed heartily.

Clearly God's Spirit was at work in Dit's heart. A few weeks later he came alone to the house, this time with drooping shoulders. He spoke hesitatingly. "I resigned my position as senior student at school today."

I waited for him to continue.

"I can't recite the prayers of veneration to the Buddha anymore, since I have believed in Jesus." Struggling for composure, he continued, "When I told the headmaster, he said, 'If that is so, then you may no longer lead the school in singing the national anthem or in saluting the flag.'" The high-schooler swallowed hard. "It means I will lose my scholarship too."

While I thanked God for giving Dit the conviction and courage to confess Jesus Christ openly, I knew he was hurting. The words of his respected headmaster had cut deeply. I shared his hurt, and together we turned to God's Word and searched for promises that would encourage, comfort, and build faith. We prayed, thanking God for joy in salvation and asking for faith for Dit to live for Jesus.

When Dit left, his shoulders had straightened again. I watched him as he strode up the lane and prayed silently, *O Lord, may he find that place of refuge under the shadow of Your wings—the place many of us have found in times of testing!* ■

ಶ 25 ೞ

Piercing
the Darkness

A fter his decision to follow Christ, Dit repeatedly asked us to visit his grandmother. "She's the one who reared me," he said, "and I want her to know about Jesus too."

In April, during the hot-season school holiday, the opportunity came. Along miles of dry back-country roads, Dit and I and a fellow worker jostled in a springless bus that threw up huge clouds of dust. At a narrow river we transferred to a motor-propelled dugout. Oiled rags plugged numerous holes in the floor. Those plugs, plus Dit's zealous bailing, kept us afloat until we reached the home of one of his aunts.

The aunt's family welcomed us with hot tea and delicious sweet bean-and-rice cakes, wrapped and steamed in banana leaves. From there we walked across newly harvested rice fields to the house of Dit's grandmother. "You *will* tell them about Jesus, won't you?" the slender lad implored. "This is a good opportunity because Uncle has just finished the new extension to our house, and he's invited lots of people to a housewarming and merit-making ceremony tonight."

Dit seemed especially eager for us to meet his grandmother and tell her about God and the wonderful salvation he had found in Jesus. Disappointment showed on his face when she sat with us only a few minutes before bustling off to help with food preparations for over one hundred expected guests.

Throughout the afternoon Dit led us from one house to another in the little community. After introductions at each place, he would say, "Now tell them about Jesus!"

The friendly listeners asked us to explain the colorful Gospel posters we had brought. They also urged us to play, over and over again on our portable phonograph, the records that explained how our world was created and the way of deliverance from sin's penalty through Jesus Christ.

Later at the grandmother's house freely flowing local toddy and rice wine turned up the volume of talk and laughter, making quiet talks difficult. Once we had eaten of his grandmother's feast, Dit led us to another home away from the raucous band and noisy revelers. There he gathered a few who wanted to know more. We sat around a smoking carbide lamp, answering questions from God's Word. Others dropped by, listened for a while, then left. Some stretched out on the floor behind us and went to sleep. Three or four remained, probing for answers.

Near midnight, when some of the drunken merry-makers staggered into the room where we sat still in discussion, we thought it prudent to leave. Following Dit to the home of yet another aunt, we found mat-tresses, with sheets—a very special consideration—already prepared for us. The unceasing clamor and a pounding headache kept me awake for a time. Still, I was thankful for a good day.

The next morning as we were saying goodbye to our gracious hostesses and Dit's grandmother, Dit called, "Hurry, or we will miss the early morning boat!"

Racing across the fields, we heard the sputter of a motor. As the outboard ignited, its roar drowned out Dit's shouts. We watched the boat speed away. Slow-ing our pace to catch our breath, we walked to the shade of an old tamarind tree on the bank of the river to wait for the next available rivercraft. As we sat there, we talked and thanked God for the many opportunities He had given to share the message of Jesus with so many of Dit's family.

An hour passed before a second boat came. Re-freshed, we gratefully climbed aboard and seated ourselves on the floor for the downstream ride to a village where I had scheduled a Bible study with some leprosy patients the following day. The other two went on home.

Arriving at the house where I had arranged to spend the night, I found only a child. She seemed not to know anything about my coming. "No one will be home until evening," she said.

Concluding that I would need to go home and return the next day, I headed toward the road. As I approached it, I saw a cloud of dust billowing behind a bus as it sped toward Singburi. Grimly I realized I would have to wait another two hours for the next bus.

In the noonday sun I stood wondering what to do. Suddenly I heard a shout, "Doctor! Doctor!" I turned to see Phon, a patient of mine, running toward me. "Wherever have you been?" she exclaimed. "I've been waiting all morning for you! Auntie had to go to market today. She asked someone else to prepare for you."

Taking the picture roll and portable phonograph from my hands, she chided, "Why did you think of going home? You could have come to our house." Scolding all the way, she trotted on ahead of me to the tiny thatched hut where she and her older sister lived.

After we chatted with the sister for a time, I followed Phon to the house where I would spend the night. Four generations lived together in this large, old-Thai-style country home. The great-grandmother, in her nineties, was a wizened, bent woman with piercing eyes. Her daughter, the organizer of the home, had a puffy face that I guessed resulted from a common vitamin B deficiency. An energetic thirty-year-old and a sweet ten-year-old completed the family. A cousin and his wife, who served the family as farm hands, also lived in the home.

When my hostesses suggested a bath, I accepted

gratefully. Phon led the way to the river. "White folk don't do things like the Thai," she commented to the ten-year-old. She discovered, though, that I could bathe in the river with no greater mishap than losing my bar of slippery soap in the slime at my feet. Great-granddaughter dived to retrieve it from between my toes.

Phon returned to her own home. The no-longer-shy youngster led me back to the cool, shaded house. For the rest of the pleasant afternoon, the oldest and youngest members of the household entertained me while others busied themselves with evening work.

As shadows lengthened, I heard the crackle of fire and smelled the spicy aroma of cooking food. Before long a large, round enamel tray with bowls of fresh-fried vegetables, scrambled eggs, fish sauce, and steamed rice appeared and was set on the floor beside me. In accordance with the polite custom of the time, they left me, their guest, to eat alone. Aware that the food on the tray would feed the whole family, I helped myself to a generous portion of rice—always in abundance—but partook sparingly of the savory eggs and vegetables.

After the evening chores, I went to the river with others for another bath. Refreshed and clean, the family sat around the big tray for their evening meal. While they ate, the great-grandmother asked me to play the records on the phonograph for the others to hear, as I had done for her throughout the afternoon.

Darkness drew on. The family, now weary and ready for rest, unrolled individual mats onto the cool

208 A Promise Is to Keep

floor and lay down. I did the same on a mat spread for me near the grandmother. After the older woman had blown out the light, she sat for a long time musing aloud about the things she had heard. *Is the Spirit moving in her heart?* I wondered. *May it be so, Lord!* I prayed.

Tired and truly thankful for the open, sincere welcome in this home, I hardly noticed that only a thin straw mat lay between me and the polished wooden floor. Drifting off to sleep, I felt deeply the privilege of being God's messenger to that home. ■

ಖ26ಞ

New Assignment

*P*rayer, painstaking study, and persistent use
gradually made the Thai language mine. Practical experience and the counsel of leprosy specialists helped me gain confidence in caring for patients. Neighborhood children responded eagerly to our Bible studies and interest in our English classes grew. Encouraged in my work and increasingly identifying with the people, I began to feel truly at home.

The doctor in charge of our central Thailand leprosy program surveyed the region and encouraged me to open a clinic among needy people in a neighboring area. With support from local missionaries, the work in the new clinic—my seventh—developed rapidly. Many came in those early days who did not have leprosy, but needed the same careful examination and reassurance as those who did. I found the challenge gratifying.

*T*he new clinic had been operating only a few months when a letter came from mission headquarters in Singapore asking if I would consider filling the position of nursing team leader at an OMF hospital taking shape in south Thailand. The letter came as a jolt. Though I had once thought that hospital nursing would be my sphere of service, my reassignment to leprosy work had completely changed my thinking. Working with physically and socially disadvantaged leprosy sufferers had so satisfied me that I now had no desire to return to institutional nursing.

The site of the new hospital lay five hundred miles to the south, only sixty miles north of the Malayan border. Eighty percent of the people living in the area were ethnic Malays. Though Thai citizens, they had a distinct and very different culture, language, and religion. Accepting the invitation to work there would almost mean starting over again. Could I—should I—consider a third big change? I was nearly forty. What if I failed in this new endeavor?

As I prayed, I knew the issue was not my ability—but whether this proposed change was God's plan for me. Time and again the Lord had marvelously helped me in difficult assignments when I totally yielded to His will. Realizing this, I ignored the reluctance of my heart and asked Him to show me how to respond. His answer came in the words He spoke long ago to Gideon: "Go in this thy might...have not I sent thee?" (Judges 6:14, KJV). Assured of God's unfailing faithfulness, I wrote my letter of acceptance.

I found it wrenchingly painful to pull up deep roots

and say goodbye again to patients and friends in central Thailand. But confident of God's leading in this new change, I found peace.

As our train sped down Thailand's lush, green peninsula, its click-clacking wheels seemed to repeat those words of promise over and over: "Go in this thy might, this thy might, this thy might...have I not sent thee, I sent thee, I sent thee?" The words encouraged me, quieted trepidation, and helped ease the pain of separation.

A friendly dental student and her grandfather, seated across the aisle from me, added enjoyment to the journey by explaining the sights from the window. Moving out of Bangkok, we passed scores of neatly planted vegetable gardens, pineapple farms, fruit orchards, and groves of sugar palms. Farther along, the tracks hugged the eastern seashore. Then, turning inland, we climbed into mountains mantled in jungle, scarred only by towering rocks. Still farther south, we passed open tin mines and mile after mile of luxuriant rubber plantations and coconut groves. I began to hear the different language among throngs of colorfully dressed Malays on station platforms. Domed Muslim mosques took the place of gilded Buddhist temples.

At journey's end one of the clinic doctors met me. From the taxi I had my first glimpse of the town of Saiburi. Shimmering heatwaves rose from sandy streets and lanes. Tall palms and shady old fruit trees swayed gently above tile rooftops. Unpainted shop-front homes along the main street reminded me of

Old China, except that here the shopkeepers included not only Chinese, but also Malays, Indians, and Thai.

"Well, here we are!" announced the doctor as our taxi pulled to a stop before one of the two-story shop-front buildings.

I had turned toward raucous music coming from a gaudy theater across the street when I heard my name. Members of the medical team piled out the front door of the little mission clinic to greet me. Curious patients behind them strained to see what all the excitement was about. What a welcome!

Later I unpacked in my first Saiburi home, an old Thai-style house on stilts just around the corner.

Three quarters of a mile away, in the shadow of a towering lighthouse, the new hospital was rising on the white sands. Nearby the weathered homes of fisherfolk huddled in the shade of graceful coconut palms. Seeing it for the first time, I recalled a letter I had received up north. The business letter concluded lightly, "Having been to Saiburi for a brief visit, I know what compensations await you. Blue lagoons, rolling surf, and sea bathing is hardly your lot in central Thailand. You'll have to be careful when you write your first circular letter from south Thailand, or it may sound like a tourist brochure!"

Now I knew what the writer meant. I had come to a true tropical paradise. That first night at Saiburi I prayed, "Lord, please don't let all this beauty become commonplace to me." God answered that prayer.

But I discovered another side to that idyllic spot in

the years that followed. Battling for lives and souls in the little hospital, we saw ugly, corrupting things perpetrated by those who cared for neither life nor property. Faced with that dark side, I learned to pray, "Oh, Lord, don't let these sordid things blind my eyes or numb my heart to the deep needs of those who come to us. You brought me here. Help me to be what You want me to be and to do what You want me to do...in Your might."

God heard that prayer too. ■

ఇ27ఇ
Almost from Scratch Again

Helping start another rural hospital in Thailand, this time at Saiburi, in some ways mirrored my earlier experience at Manorom. In many ways it did not. Certainly planning and organizing *things* came more easily. But sorting out *people* problems that resulted from south Thailand's multiple languages and cultures added a new dimension! I often needed the advice of the team who had served many years in the town clinic. Our times of unhurried prayer and consultation helped immensely. I shall always be grateful as well that I had four *months* to prepare instead of four *weeks*.

In the mid-forties and fifties, few rural public schools in Thailand offered more than a four-year curriculum, with all subjects taught in Thai. Since many Malay children, especially the girls, spoke little Thai, they were not encouraged to attend Thai schools. This complicated the selection and training of national helpers for work in our hospital.

Though most local inhabitants could get along at the market, they could not communicate comprehensively in the other group's language. I struggled with Malay myself, but also with the differences in the southern Thai dialect. Until we worked out helpful guidelines, verbal miscues created hilarious, even embarrassing situations.

Basic nursing textbooks being unavailable, we had to write, translate, and duplicate our own materials. We also compiled—in Thai, Malay, and English—a list of terms, including body parts, symptoms, diseases, treatments, hospital equipment, medical and surgical supplies, and departments.

As another of my pre-opening tasks, I oriented cleaners, laundresses, and gardeners to their new jobs. That, too, challenged my ingenuity. Women hired as cleaners had to learn to sweep and mop floors. At home they simply brushed back and forth with a soft broom until dust and sand fell through the cracks, then hand-wiped the floor with an old, damp cloth. Hospital floors had no cracks, and maneuvering wide sponge mops around beds, stools, and bedside lockers seemed to them ridiculously awkward.

Laundresses who had always done the family wash in a basin of cold water by the well or at the riverside now faced not only scrubbing hospital linens and uniforms by hand, but also doing the unbelievable extra step of *boiling* them. Once they had mastered the hand wringer, though, they delighted in demonstrating the technique to curious onlookers. Everyone in rubber country had seen similar machines press latex rubber, but never clothes!

Gardeners believed they should pull out all grass and weeds so that they could rake the dry sand into fancy swirls and patterns to confuse and keep the snakes at bay! They were slow to concede that regularly cut grass could be as snake free—and cooler.

Gradually our employees grew accustomed to our strange ways and we to theirs!

With opening scheduled for January 1, 1960, we set the day before Christmas as the last day for the old clinic in town. In the intervening days new employees, using hired trucks, helped shift equipment from the clinic to the new location. By New Year's Eve the hospital had a surprisingly "ready" look.

New Year's Day, guests and visitors gathered under cloudless skies and listened with quiet attention to the speeches and prayers and waited expectantly for the unveiling of the nameplate, which read, HOSPITAL CHRISTIAN SAIBURI. Later they toured the hospital, gazing admiringly—some a bit fearfully—at strange and shining equipment.

One visitor, well known to all who had worked at the clinic, was eager to see everything. He entered the operating room with one of the doctors. With a playful gesture, the man sprang onto the operating table. Clutching his abdomen, he lay groaning. "All right," doctor, you may operate now," he jested.

The doctor, responding to the man's prank,

pumped the table to its highest position. "Just like an airplane ride!" the delighted clown exclaimed as he jumped to the floor. Ironically, a year later, while away from Saiburi, this man died of a ruptured appendix.

For me the most satisfying moment of that happy day was helping thirteen teenaged girls button crisp, white aprons over new blue uniforms. During the weeks of preliminary training, they had endeared themselves to me. I enjoyed introducing them to some of the mysteries of the human body and teaching them basic principles for the care of the sick and injured. But telling them about the God who created our bodies was the greatest privilege.

In spite of notices in Thai, Chinese, and Malay pasted on the doors of the old clinic, some patients took a long time to discover where the foreign doctors had gone. The delay gave everyone time to adjust to new duties in unfamiliar surroundings.

I had delegated the oversight of aides in the wards and outpatient departments to other OMF nurses. I launched aides in the operating rooms and sterile supplies department. Teaching the meaning and necessity of "sterile" cleanness took watchful perseverance. Undoubtedly this gave birth to my nickname, *"Mother Pineapple,"* from the fact that a pineapple has eyes on all sides!

One evening I had gone back to the autoclave room to redo a load of inadequately sterilized goods, when the night watchman came to find me. "Come," he said, "a couple of jeep-loads of people have just arrived."

Going to the front of the hospital, I found a middle-aged man, his face ashen, slumped in a jeep. Anxious relatives surrounded him. It was not unusual for whole families to accompany patients—neighbors sometimes just came along for an outing. This time it looked as if the whole village had come!

We extracted the man from the vehicle and moved him into the admitting room. There the doctor quickly administered oxygen to relieve his acute distress.

While taking the man's history, we learned that he had made the pilgrimage to Mecca. That made him a highly respected community leader and accounted for the crowd. Also during admission I observed that our new patient tried to keep one foot hidden. Immediately I recognized symptoms I had often seen in my leprosy clinics.

A few days later, when I went to do dressings on his foot, the man asked, "Tell me, what are these sores? Why won't they heal? I've had them ever since a snake bit me over twenty years ago. That's why my two toes are missing."

While listening to his tale, I cleansed the deep wounds and snipped away dead, unfeeling tissue around the crusted ulcers. I wondered if he really didn't know the reason for them. He pulled himself up to a sitting position to watch me work. After a time, in broken English, he asked, "Is this le-pre-see?"

Impossible to evade his direct, earnest question, I replied, "Yes, it is."

The proud community leader sank back onto the

bed and cried like a child, doubtless relieving years of anxious torment. He then turned to his two wives seated on the floor beside his bed. Speaking in Malay, he told them what I had said.

Turning again to me, he asked, "Did you know what I had when you let me come into your hospital the other night?"

When I told him that I did, he choked out the words, "For years I have wanted to come to see the foreign doctors, but I feared that if they knew I had leprosy, they would turn me away. Now I know they wouldn't have. Do you suppose this was the reason for my heart attack—so that I could come here and really find out?"

"We welcome all who come to our hospital," I said—adding that for several years I had worked with leprosy sufferers.

The man lay quietly reflecting for a while. Then half to his wives and half for my benefit, he said, "I knew if they really believed in Jesus and their religion, as they say they do, they wouldn't send me away. Now I know it's true!"

The man remained in the hospital for three weeks. During that time he asked many questions about Jesus. Yet, like so many who came to us, he was zealous for a religion that recognizes Jesus as a great prophet, but denies that He is the Son of God. We had come to Saiburi to proclaim Jesus Christ as Lord and Savior to just such people. ■

Costly Choices

We started each morning at the hospital with short devotions and prayer for the work of the day. Those who chose not to come were expected to be at work. During their preliminary training, incoming trainees began their day with devotions simply because they had not yet been assigned to hospital duties. Those morning devotions gave most girls from Buddhist or Muslim backgrounds their first introduction to Jesus Christ.

Invariably some in each new group of trainees told us they would like to follow Jesus. Fear and family opposition kept most from continuing on to know Him.

One trainee, Nee, made it quite clear from the first that she was *un*interested. During devotions she disturbed those around her by giggling and whispering. In the wards she found devious ways to keep others from listening to the gospel messages broadcast daily throughout the hospital. We prayed earnestly for that teenager. Gradually—in spite of willful, studied opposition—she began to ask searching questions.

Nee had been with us nearly a year when fellow OMF missionaries held a series of evangelistic meetings in an unused theater across the street from the hospital. I rearranged work schedules for the aides who asked to attend. Nee did not ask.

During that week the local spirit doctor, who strongly opposed our Christian witness, entered the ward where Nee worked. In mock surprise he asked, "And why didn't you go over to learn how to be a Christian?"

"I don't need to," Nee responded. "I already know,"

"What are you saying, child?" the man retorted. "Don't tell me you have swallowed the foreigners' religion!"

"I have," she responded quietly and left the room.

Cutting short his visit, the scoffer went directly to the village elders. Some of them had earlier declared that the foreign doctors were welcome in the village, but their religion was not. "Have you heard?" the angry man blurted out. "The daughter of one of our officials has disgraced her worthy family and betrayed our country!"

At home that night, when Nee's Buddhist parents asked about the matter, Nee acknowledged the decision she had made to follow Jesus. Her parents reacted more mildly than she expected. "We have seen great changes in your life lately," they said. "Now we know the reason! Though we cannot fully approve your decision, we will not forbid it either."

The next day Nee shared the news and her joy at morning prayers. The bells rang not only in heaven, but in our hearts as we praised God together for answering prayer for this once willful young woman.

M oh, from a Muslim home, had a very different story. She came gladly to morning devotions, listened attentively, and obviously enjoyed the singing. One day she asked if she might borrow a hymnbook. "I'd like to copy the words of 'Guide Me, O Thou Great Jehovah.'" she said, "I want to pin them on the wall in my room at home."

Moh continued to come to devotions even after preliminary training. Then one day I missed her. Later she came to find me to explain that her uncle had forbidden her ever to attend prayers again. With tears she said, "He has torn my hymn from the wall and threatened to remove me from training. May I stay even if I don't come to prayers?" she asked.

"Of course, you may," I assured her.

Some days later I inquired how things were going for her at home. Bursting into tears, she answered, "Every day when I get home, Uncle questions and threatens me. He has even asked one of the other employees here to keep an eye on me to see that I do not go to prayers or listen to what you say about Jesus. If I do, he says he will beat me. I know he will too."

Months later the girl came asking to live at the hospital. "A little room, just anywhere, so I won't have to live at Uncle's," she begged.

We had no room. The student dormitory was still only on the drawing board. When we finally built it, Moh was among the first to move in.

Later Moh married and moved from the hospital compound. Though she continued to work with us several years, she walked a tortuous road. She came often for counsel, telling us of her longing still to follow Jesus. Fearful threats and cunning lies kept her from fully committing herself to Him.

Because of our daily public witness to Jesus at the hospital, the opposition of Moh's family to her continuing in our employ mounted. Their aggravated torment and pitiless pressure pushed Moh to mental confusion and finally breakdown. No longer able to cope, she left the hospital.

The young woman's family took her to both Muslim and Buddhist mediums. In their rituals they pressed her into involvement with spirits. Deeply depressed and sometimes physically ill, Moh was brought back to the hospital for treatment. When they did, family members never left her alone, even for a minute, resisting any mention of the name of Jesus.

When I saw Moh last, her once bright, lovely face darkened as she spoke of her special ability to help the sick. "I give them injections, just like you taught us. Then I call on my guardian spirits to heal and to keep them."

To this day I grieve for Moh. ■

ඬ29ଓ

Promise Tested

One afternoon I glumly made my way to the classroom. My students had not done well on an exam. To some extent, their inadequate answers reflected *my* failure to explain the subject material clearly in Thai.

A shout interrupted my thoughts just as I reached the door. "Teacher! Teacher! Come quickly! A truck has just arrived with lots of people from a dreadful accident."

Motioning to the waiting students to follow, I hurried to the admitting area. We found appalling chaos. Two overloaded buses full of drunken guests had been returning from a wedding feast. Passengers had challenged the drivers to race. Their broken, bleeding bodies were now being delivered to our hospital.

We immediately began helping the injured to the admitting area as vehicle after vehicle arrived with casualties. Stranded survivors, anxious relatives, and curious onlookers mobbed the hospital corridors. Pushing open windows and doors to watch, they made it nearly impossible for us to perform our urgent tasks.

Discouragement about my students vanished as I watched them responding capably to the needs of doctors, nurses, and moaning passengers. We examined and treated more than thirty people that frenzied afternoon, admitting seven of the most seriously injured to the wards.

Hospital policy required that one relative or friend stay with each inpatient at all times, day and night, throughout the person's hospital stay. For each of the seven gravely injured that day, we permitted two.

*I*n the next few hours a nightmare unfolded. During the night some of the friends and relatives of the injured began threatening the missionary nurses and young trainees with obscene language and gestures. Because it put the safety of our personnel at risk, we considered this behavior intolerable. In the morning— after prayerful consideration and agonizing—we discharged all seven new patients.

Never again would we have to take such action. Not only did the community support our response, but God protected us from revenge.

We did not come away from that deplorable episode unscathed, however. Although not actually involved in the conflict, our newest missionary nurse found the night's stress so traumatic that she left Thailand and returned to her homeland.

Y ears later another unforgettable confrontation with evil began during a happy occasion—the wedding feast of one of our senior nurse aides. Our nursing instructor, Marjorie Nowell, and I had been honored with seats at the bridal table. In the midst of the evening's festivities a disturbance at the edge of the crowd drew our attention to a classmate of the bride. She shoved her way toward us. Planting herself directly in front of the nursing instructor, she began cursing loudly. Slanderously she accused Marjorie of trying to force her to become a Christian. The bridal couple and others at the table listened in horror.

Praying for wisdom and protection from the adversary, I edged up to the angry girl. Speaking quietly, I led her away. As we crossed the road to the Buddhist temple grounds where the hospital jeep was parked, the girl began resisting me. She tried to pull me toward the temple, insisting we go there and that I bow to the idol.

Holding her arm securely with one hand and praying silently, I gradually guided my unwilling ward toward the jeep. Once beside the open vehicle, I locked my free arm around the door frame and nodded to the driver, who stood fearfully at a distance. He and others from the hospital now came to help the sullen aide into the vehicle. Silent, wild-eyed, and with foaming mouth, she spat at me the entire eight-mile drive back to the hospital.

At the hospital we called for her family. An older brother, whom we later learned was an ardent temple devotee, came for her. Speaking harshly to his sister, he pushed her roughly onto the back of his motorbike and roared away.

Later, when we dismissed the girl from our employment, God kept the brother from carrying out his threats of reprisal.

Both before and after this encounter with the forces of evil, the fierceness of the struggle tempted me to give up. I was responsible for filling the seemingly endless gaps left by staff losses and transfers. Sometimes need pressured me to call nurses new to Thailand and still in basic language study to help for limited periods of time. Although they tried valiantly to cope with everything new and strange in our little hospital, these new missionaries needed more encouragement than I could give them. All felt the stretch and strain of such times.

For me weariness and ongoing taunts of the enemy heightened my sense of inadequacy. *See what a mess you are making of things!* the adversary whispered. *If you would leave, others could make it. You are the problem. If you went, God could really work here.*

One morning, in deep anguish, I wondered how I could make it through another day. I needed a break. With no opportunity for time off, I felt trapped.

I glanced at the clock and wondered if I had time for a quick run to the beach, only a ten-minute walk away.

Yes, I decided, *I have time.* I picked up a copy of *Daily Light* and a couple of bananas and quietly slipped away from the sleeping household.

Yesterday's waves had carved tiny cliffs in the sand. I selected a shallow cove and settled down, my back to the hospital and its problems. Munching on a banana, I watched for sunrise.

I tried to pray, but fatigued and depressed, I began to sob instead. At that moment I felt like helpless prey in the mouth of the "roaring lion." The day before three of my best senior aides had laid letters of resignation on my desk. A few days earlier, angry accusations of favoritism had violently shaken me. Not many days before that the shocking discovery of unfaithfulness in a trusted member of staff had left me numb. Each time I tried to break free of discouragement and get on my feet, I was trounced and pummeled again.

As I sat in my misery, the sun burst from the sea. For a brief moment, shining clear, it sent a glorious, shimmering path across the water to my feet. In another moment it slipped behind skyline haze and clouds, but in those few seconds, God penetrated to the depths of my dispirited heart. *I am with you, even though clouds and haze may sometimes hide My face,* He encouraged me.

Through tears I reached for my book. I do not remember the Scripture portions I read that morning, but I do remember I resolved anew to keep my promise—made so many years before—to the One whose promises never fail.

As it was nearly duty time, I hurried back to the hospital. Encouraged, I knew I could, and, by His grace, I would go on. ■

∞30∝
Tried by Terror

In the midst of our busy hospital routine we became increasingly aware that our once quiet community had changed into an arena for spine-tingling atrocities. Victims from despicable acts of terrorism filled our beds. Sometimes the Thai army brought their wounded for emergency care until they could be air-lifted to military facilities. The surgical staff spent tedious hours searching ragged wounds for bullets, stitching nasty knife- or ax-inflicted wounds or picking charred debris from horrible burns. In a single year three of our nurse's aides lost their fathers to terrorist violence.

No longer unusual, the chilling sound of gunfire rang in the streets. The reach of terror inched closer.

One early morning a faithful employee came to my door. With tremulous voice he asked, "Did you hear the shooting last night?" I nodded. "It was at my house," he said.

The man told this remarkable story: "My son Ooh and I had just come from our baths in the river, and I had sat down to read the Bible. Ooh had been standing across the table from me, but then came and sat on my knee. That's when bullets came through, splintering the back wall." Pausing to gain control, he continued, "If Ooh had stayed where he stood minutes before, at the other side of the table, he would have been killed. God protected us, didn't he?"

With my hand on his shoulder, I waited as he wept unashamedly. "Yes, the Lord surely watched over you," I said. "Let's thank Him."

After we prayed the shaken man asked for time off to repair his house. I gave it to him.

A few evenings later the man's wife, in great agitation, came to see me. "What shall we do now?" she cried. "The terrorists are demanding big protection money." Handing me the extortion note, she continued, "We don't have money like that. They told me where I must go tonight to pay it. Do you think I should?" Her eyes showed her terror. "My husband says we need to trust God. But if I don't go, they may do something even worse, like kidnapping one of us."

In such situations, we found counselling difficult. Anything we said was easily countered with, "But you don't understand. You have never been threatened as we have." We came to understand.

One dark midnight I was startled from sleep when an automatic weapon dumped a round of bullets into our hospital compound. I sprang from bed. I heard no cries, only oppressive silence. Then from the dormitory above a student whispered urgently, "Mother! Teacher! What was that?"

"Shhh!" I cautioned. "Be quiet until we hear activity elsewhere!" Presently we saw the hospital superintendent guardedly descend the steps of his house and hurry to the hospital. He checked on anxious staff and patients, then notified the police from our only phone to the outside.

Happily, the bullets had inflicted no injuries in the hospital. But, as instructed, we remained indoors and away from windows until morning light. I joined the students upstairs.

At daybreak the compound came alive with police, patients' relatives, friends and neighbors. I wondered if, among the milling crowd, an innocent-looking extortionist gathered information. No one could know.

A nest of empty cartridges found on the far side of the swamp behind the hospital revealed the terrorists' vantage point. Only one bullet had reached the hospital. Many others, however, had penetrated the single-thickness clapboard walls of our staff houses. Miraculously no one inside was hurt.

The most amazing stories of God's protection came from the graduate nurse's aides, whose home had taken the major assault. Two aides who came off duty at eleven had been relaxing over cups of hot chocolate before retiring. They had gone to their rooms only seconds before three bullets passed at head level over the sofa where they had been sitting. Those bullets had come through an outside wall, whizzing only inches from where an aide lay asleep on her bed. In that same room two other bullets passed through the pillow of an aide who had gone on duty an hour earlier. In the next room a sixth bullet had ricocheted off the bedpost, barely missing another sleeping aide.

I marveled, rejoicing in God's sovereign control over those lethal missiles. As I gathered into my arms those He had so graciously protected, I wept in thanksgiving.

Three days after that terrifying burst of gunfire we received *our* protection-money demand. It was actually our second extortion letter. The first had come two weeks before. We had refused to answer or comply.

After that second letter our field leaders called the hospital staff together and explained our mission's policy. We could not and would not pay extortion demands for any felony.

We gave our employees the opportunity of temporary leave with full pay until we could see how the matter would settle. Contacting the parents of our newest trainees, we asked that they come and take their daughters home until conditions were safer.

Nearly all of the permanent staff remained at their jobs. God drew us closer to one another as we confirmed our trust that He would keep us from further incident.

Now we could truly empathize with those who daily faced the dreadful terror of similar threats. ∎

ஃ31ஃ
Patch of Blue Sky

After the shooting, government-assigned police guards became part of daily life around the hospital. In fact, we began to see uniformed personnel everywhere we went. Highways sprouted roadblocks and checkpoints.

Terrorism exacted a horrible toll in south Thailand. Many suffered. Casualties continued to fill many of our beds.

Into that stormy unrest and darkness God sent us a bright patch of blue sky in a most unusual way. The Thai Marines and the U.S. Navy had set up a base for joint exercises a few miles to the north of us. One afternoon a jeep-load of Navy personnel arrived at our hospital gates. They had come with an invitation for our staff to visit their field hospital. "We will send vehicles for you," the officers promised. Our compound buzzed with excitement.

We rearranged duties so that different groups

could go on separate days. Each group returned with
enthusiastic reports of all they had seen and done.
"They welcomed us and gave us a wonderful tour,"
gushed a spokesman for one group. "Their hospital is
all in tents! And—do you know what?—we have lots
of things just like theirs. They even call them by the
same names!" Obviously their visit had not only been
a fun outing, but a learning experience as well.

In return our doctors invited the military men to our
hospital. As maneuvers permitted, scores of sailors
and marines came. They showed as much amazement
at our compact facility by the sea as our staff had
expressed about their sprawling tents on the beach.
"We never imagined such a place out here," various
soldiers commented. Others expressed wistful interest
in our work. "Some day I'd like to do something like
this," said one.

A senior officer being shown through the hospital
asked what diseases we found most common and the
kinds of surgery we did. "What about dentistry?" he
asked. "Do you have a dental clinic?"

"No, we do only simple extractions," the OMF
doctor escorting him replied. "We certainly have a
need, but we have no dentist."

"In that case," the officer asked, "would you like
our ship's dentist to give you a hand? He hasn't much
to do right now and would be glad to help for a few
days."

That kind offer resulted in our once-only dental
clinic at the hospital. The navy dentist and his assis-

tant brought portable equipment from the ship and treated over forty people in the two and a half days they worked with us.

One of our nurse's aides, with an impacted wisdom tooth, needed equipment that could not be brought ashore. So the Navy moved the ship to the mouth of our river and ferried the girl out for surgery!

That aide was the envy of all. Oh, to have an impacted tooth! Aware of the hankering of others for a visit, the dentist received permission from his senior officer for any of our staff "in uniform" to board the ship for a look-see. Without the "uniform" stipulation, the whole village might have gone!

Before the fleet steamed away, they brought us generous gifts. Pharmacy shelves groaned under bottles of vitamins, tonics, lotions, and powders. We used cash gifts to cover the cost of surgery or medicines for poor patients. Tins of food and candy and boxes of toys we tucked away for our annual Christmas party.

One donation I wondered about, though—cartons of intravenous solutions stacked from floor to ceiling. When would we ever use *a hundred quarts* of IV normal saline?

I needn't have wondered. Our heavenly Father had it all planned. About a month after the Navy left, a raging cholera epidemic swept into our area. To care for the numbers, we turned a seven-bed ward into an isolation unit and gave bottle after bottle of that life-sustaining fluid to desperately dehydrated patients. We quickly used up those one hundred bottles of intravenous solution—but not before additional stock came in.

Lives would certainly have been lost without that ready and ample supply of IV solution. As it was, we did not lose one patient in the epidemic, nor did any of our heavily taxed staff contract the disease. I thanked God for a dedicated staff, and even more for His marvelous "pre-provision" of those bottles of plain old normal saline!

Not only is our God faithful, but He delights to throw in "extras"—those patches of blue sky—to encourage us. ■

❧32❧
Kidnapped!

Waves of terrorist activity swept across Thailand's southernmost provinces. With each crushing breaker came new and stifling restraints. Automatic weapons in hand, the police assigned to guard the hospital now accompanied our vehicles whenever they traveled outside the village. We could no longer transport dying patients or corpses back to country homes. We were urged not even to visit the rural homes of our national staff.

Trips to neighboring cities to purchase hospital and household supplies we kept to a minimum. Instead, we bought things from local merchants or ordered them through truck drivers known to have paid "protection money." By late afternoons the "Asian Highway," which passed just a mile from our village, was deserted.

Restrictions also robbed us of recreation. We could no longer enjoy outings to a beautiful nearby waterfall. Nor when the moon was full, could we go with our young people to the beach for fun evenings of hunting and frying crabs. Authorities advised us not to go to the beach at all, except in broad daylight and only in large groups.

The ugly side of our tropical paradise was becoming more evident.

One hot mid-morning in April the swinging doors to my office flung open, revealing the X-ray assistant. "Minka and Margaret have been kidnapped!" he said, steadying himself.

The police had just called to notify the hospital of the nurses' abduction. The shattering news reverberated through the corridors. Horror clutched at our hearts and settled over the hospital.

Minka and Margaret were our co-workers, our friends. Both had worked at the hospital in Saiburi until they joined the team of itinerant leprosy workers. Minka Hanskamp, tall, slim, and gray-haired, came to Thailand from the Netherlands. Margaret Morgan, shorter, dark-haired, and a poet, was from Wales.

That morning the two women had gone to one of their rural clinics about sixty miles from Saiburi. As they prepared to treat the patients who had gathered, a taxi arrived. Two men strode to the simple shelter and asked if the nurses would come immediately to see some very sick people. Minka and Margaret agreed to go as soon as they had seen the waiting patients.

Suddenly turning, the intruders brandished

weapons. They seized the two nurses and ordered them to the taxi. Covering the women's heads with burlap bags, the kidnappers pushed them into the cab and sped away.

The hospital superintendent dispatched the terrible information to our local field leader. From there the news flashed to OMF directors and to praying people around the world. Collectively we held our breath, waiting for further developments.

Three days after the kidnapping, a letter arrived, anonymously delivered to the hospital. It demanded an outrageous ransom with international involvement. Waves of horror swept over the four gathered in my apartment to read it. Contrary to the hopes of some who saw the kidnapping and heard the abductors' words, Minka and Margaret had not been taken to care for sick and injured out in the mountains. They were hostages.

We all knew of our mission's policy not to pay ransom. Paralyzing fears clawed at our hearts. We turned to God in prayer, our only *sure* recourse. My heart broke especially for Minka, who as a girl had suffered captivity in Indonesia under the Japanese. Her father had died there in a concentration camp.

Without the enduring promises from God's Word, our team of local missionaries surely would have foundered. To say I never feared during those desolate days would be a lie. But God patiently sought to teach each of us the meaning of Christ's words to His disciples when they were fearful and questioning: "Peace I leave with you, my peace I give to you; not as the world gives do I give to you. Let not your heart be troubled, neither let it be afraid" (Jn. 14:27, NKJV). "These things I have spoken to you, that *in me* you may have peace. In the world you will have tribulation; but...I have overcome the world" (Jn. 16:33, NKJV). We claimed those words for ourselves and for Minka and Margaret out in the jungle.

Mission leaders urged us to continue our work as normally as possible. We tried, but the nurses in captivity never left our thoughts and prayers. Those troubling days and nights were, without doubt, the most difficult I have experienced.

*F*or some time after the abduction heart-wrenching communiqués, obviously dictated, came from Minka and Margaret. Despite constant prayer and unflagging efforts to obtain the women's release, contacts grew fewer and fewer. After five months they ceased completely.

One night during those long months I awakened and, as I had so often done, began to pray. Strangely enveloped in an aura of peace, I could not continue asking for our nurses' release. In my heart I felt an unexplained assurance that all was well with Minka and Margaret. Unusual as the feeling was, I lay back down and went to sleep.

Rumors, both good and ill, continued into the new year. Then one day we learned that someone had found remains near a deserted terrorist camp in the mountains. They were later confirmed to be those of Minka and Margaret.

A few days after that announcement, our male nurse came to my door. "Would you like to talk to someone who says he knew the man who killed the two nurses?" he asked.

Unsure how to respond, I asked him to call the hospital superintendent. When Dr. John Toop came, the two of us decided to meet the person with the information.

The man ushered into my office was staying with his elderly grandmother in the ward. He explained he had once been a terrorist, but disillusioned, he had deserted, and the government had granted him amnesty. He told how one evening when he returned from a raid, a fellow marauder casually announced, "Well, I shot the foreigners today."

Our informant continued: "When I asked him why he had killed them, he replied, 'The chief did not want them around during the fast month. But, you know, they were good women. They asked to pray to their God first. I shot them while they were kneeling.'" The man before us paused, then added, "I am sorry."

We asked no more. Dr. John accompanied the man from the room. When the two had gone, I closed the door and turned the key. Immediately I went to the file where I kept the previous year's work schedules. Those schedules confirmed the dates of the last Muslim fast. Ramadan began the middle of September.

Could the night I awakened, sensing that all was well with Minka and Margaret have been the evening of their execution? Surely that had been the day of their true release from villainous captivity to a glorious home in heaven. Closing the folder, I let a flood of tears flush away some of the aching anguish that had accumulated in my heart.

*H*undreds gathered for the funeral service under huge tents set up on our volleyball court. Most who came had never attended a Christian funeral. Quietly and courteously non-Christians stood with Christians listening, giving particular attention to the testimonies of two leprosy patients the murdered nurses had cared for. A Thai and a Malay, each in his own language, spoke movingly and boldly of the faith they now possessed in the Lord Jesus Christ because of the selfless devotion and loyal service of the nurses. Concluding humbly and movingly, one said, "In heaven one day we know we will see our risen Savior *and* these beloved nurses again."

Minka and Margaret did not live or die in vain. ■

ೱ33ೲ
"The King Is Coming!"

Although Saiburi was tucked away in an obscure corner of Thailand, many people visited our little hospital. Family and friends occasionally came to see where we served. Foreign-exchange students and members of the Peace Corps often popped in for inoculations or medical check-ups. Sometimes they simply wanted to talk to English-speaking people and perhaps enjoy a piece of "apple pie," made with green mangoes! "Globe-trotters" of every description gave us opportunities to show hospitality and share Christ with some curious strangers. Once an unidentified European tin-mine employee, critically ill and alone, was brought to the hospital in a taxi. His death shortly after arrival left us with some knotty problems—among them what to do with his body!

Several workmen of a Korean construction company came to worship. The first morning they showed

up I was leading the Thai Bible class. Speaking in Thai
and then translating back into English for our Korean
friends was for me a new, mentally challenging experience. But we were always glad when they came.

Once, Thailand's queen mother paid a short visit to
our village. Though she did not come to the hospital,
some of our staff glimpsed her as her limousine
stopped briefly near a welcome arch we had erected in
her honor.

T he most exciting visitors to our hospital were
    Thailand's greatly loved king, queen, and two
princesses. They came during a month-long stay at
their southern palace, not far from Saiburi.

One Sunday morning we received an invitation for
representatives from our hospital to a midday function
at the local Boy Scout camp. The king was to preside.
National staff drew numbers to determine who would
go. An Australian family, a Canadian, and an American represented our missionary staff. The group set off
happily after church for a dinner and the ceremony.
On surgery call, I could not go.

Mid-afternoon the group returned in high spirits.
Talking all at the same time, they related the wonderful things they had seen and done. "Our seats were
right near the platform, and we could see their
majesties well! Ooooh, our queen is beautiful! The
princesses smiled at us! The king liked the big photo-
graph of our river that Dr. Simpkin gave him. And—
guess what!—after dinner the royal family all came
and spoke to our group. The queen talked to the

doctor's children, and the doctor invited their majesties to visit our hospital. Do you think they will come?"

After the aides had gone to share their effervescence with others, I returned to reading. Suddenly a nurse-aide burst into my apartment. "The king is coming!" she cried.

I rushed into uniform as quickly as I ever had for any emergency and dashed to the hospital. Voices from every direction urged me, "Hurry, Mother! Hurry!"

I arrived at the front of the hospital, breathless, just in time to see two escort cars pass the end of our lane. "Oh, they are not coming after all!" rose a disappointed cry. Then a third car with flashing lights rolled nearly to a stop, turned sharply and came our way. The king's white Range Rover followed closely behind. Screams of delight rent the air: "They *are* coming! They *are* coming!"

The excited shouts subsided as the king drove slowly through our gates. A spontaneous, awed silence took over.

Our hospital superintendent, Dr. John Toop, his wife Edith, along with Dorothy Jupp, senior midwife, and I stood together to welcome the cavalcade as it drew to a stop. The doctor whispered, "Mary, you go first!"

My mouth went dry. *How do I greet a king and queen?* I thought frantically. *What do I say?*

King Bhumibol stepped from his Rover and, as though reading my mind, extended his hand. The kindly gesture put me at ease. Queen Sirikit, coming from a second vehicle, greeted me in flawless English. A truly considerate couple! I could see why they were so beloved by their people.

Dr. John escorted the king, and I accompanied the queen to visit the wards. The king, queen, or one of the princesses spoke to every patient.

When we had visited all the patients in the general wards, the king inquired about our leprosy work, indicating his desire to visit those patients as well. Some onlookers expressed dismay that the royal family would visit the leprosy ward. The leprosy patients were incredulous, but deeply moved that their king cared about them, too.

While walking back toward the front entrance of the hospital, the queen engaged Dr. Simpkin in conversation. Then, nodding to one of her aides, she took an envelope from her. Turning to the doctor, the queen handed it to him. At that very moment someone called him for an emergency. He excused himself, stuffed the envelope into his pocket, and hurried away.

While we were conducting our royal visitors through the hospital, a powerful drama unfolded at the front gate. Parents of a very sick child tried frantically to gain entrance through the throngs of people and security police. Finally, an observant attending royal physician helped get the child to the admitting room. It was too late. The child's death threw a shadow over an otherwise happy day.

We said goodbye to the royal visitors, and they

drove away. Our national staff crowded around, laughing, crying, and hugging me. "Did they like our hospital? Tell us, what did they say?" some wanted to know. "You have touched the hands of our king and queen! You won't wash your hands, now will you?" another teased as two or three clutched my hands in theirs.

*I*t *was* an exciting day. Apart from the royal visit, it was the Toops' 25th wedding anniversary and Dr. John's 60th birthday. That evening we gathered to celebrate both occasions with cake and ice cream. "By the way," I asked Dr. Simpkin, "what was in the envelope the queen gave you?"

Slapping his hip, the doctor exclaimed, "Oh, I forgot!" and drew the crumpled envelope from his pocket. Inside he found a generous gift for the hospital. With that gift we purchased two drinking fountains. Each time I passed those well-used coolers in the months and years ahead, I remembered the thrilling day when Thailand's king and queen visited us.

We thought of Minka and Margaret, still in the jungle at that time, and wished they could share our joy that day. No one felt free to speak to the king and queen about their situation. Later we learned that the king had asked local officials about them before he and his family came to the hospital.

Even now when I think back to those thrilling words, "The king is coming! The king is coming!" my heart beats faster. I think of the shout I will hear one day when the Lord Jesus Christ, the King of all kings, descends from heaven. That day He will gather from among the dead and then from the living all who have trusted in Him and take them to be with Himself forever.

Minka and Margaret will join us for that welcome day! I'm looking forward to it. ∎

ぉ34cα

The World Crowds In

Ｎews of the first moonwalk in 1969 hit our community like a meteor. People debated the event for weeks. Some dismissed the television footage as a fictitious movie. Others declared that such a thing was impossible because the Koran made no mention of man reaching the moon. Those who worshiped the sun, moon, and stars grieved. "We can no longer bow in worship or burn incense to the moon," they lamented, "because men have put their feet on it."

That historical event gave us countless opportunities to speak of the all-wise, all-powerful God, the One who made the universe with such perfect precision and timing that man's going to the moon was indeed possible.

At the same time, advances in worldwide telecommunications brought undreamed of changes to our less-advanced corner of the world. People began looking at themselves and their circumstances in a new light. Uneasy conjectures stirred the populace. We sensed a growing confusion and fear among friends and neighbors and gloomy negativism even among our hospital employees. Contentions about responsibilities and questions about work hours at the hospital made it wise to publish job descriptions and wage scales.

We became extremely grateful for a clear-headed official from the newly established government Labor Department. He kept us abreast of rapidly changing labor laws. In spite of his sharp-eyed efforts, however, on two occasions the national staff walked off their jobs. The changing world *was* crowding in.

Though Thailand did not get directly involved in the long Vietnam war, incidental fallout from the conflict would impact the nation. Five or six years after the war ended, Vietnamese refugees poured across the borders and onto Thailand's shores. Boats crossing the Gulf of Thailand from Vietnam's southwestern tip often took aim at the long stretches of isolated coastline of Thailand's southern provinces. A towering lighthouse at the mouth of the Saiburi River was undoubtedly what lured many a desperate pilot to beach his refugee-filled craft near our hospital.

Thailand was reluctant to give haven to early boatloads of refugees. If the Vietnamese crafts were still seaworthy, the coast guard towed them back out to sea. Having once been a refugee from communist oppression, I watched with deep agony.

Vessels broken and cast upon the shore, of course, could not be sent back. Though some locals living near the beach reached out to them, officials did not encourage such help. When we at the hospital learned of the Vietnamese people's misery and their whereabouts, we took them food, blankets, and clothing. Though aware of the official disapproval, we could not turn our backs on such desolation. Eventually the police and coast guard also began helping the refugees stranded on the beaches, providing shelter for some of them near our hospital.

One day an official from the United Nations Relief Organization visited us to ask if we would accept responsibility for refugees housed in an unused immigration building not far from our front gates. "We will provide funds for survival needs and nineteen cents a day per person for food," he said.

We agreed to pitch in. I found ministering to the needs of those transient people both disturbing and satisfying. Their physical bankruptcy stretched our limited material resources. But their emotional and spiritual needs presented opportunities to share friendship and the inexhaustible love and grace of our Lord Jesus. Vietnamese New Testaments and other literature obtained from the Thailand Bible Society opened doors and were always gladly received.

In nearly every group one or more of the refugees knew English well enough to make communication possible. But efforts to obtain the names, ages, and other pertinent information for police and U.N.

records inevitably triggered fear. I understood those fears. I had similar misgivings in China under repeated questionings.

Fear gave way to trust, however, as we continued our daily ministry. After a day or so elated children greeted us. Eventually even the adults welcomed our visits. That is when we began to hear of harrowing experiences at sea. Either with nostalgia or heartbreak, they also told of the more distant past in their homeland.

As rapport increased, so did our understanding of the refugees' deeper needs. Time and again I rejoiced to see God use His Word to soften hearts.

*T*wo unusually large boatloads of refugees were housed at the local police station. The day they were to be transported to a holding camp about a hundred miles up the coast I sat having my devotions in my room. In Matthew 25 I read Jesus' declaration that whatever we do to others, we do to Him. "What can I do for You today, Lord?" I asked.

Just then a policeman brought to my door a young woman refugee. Recognizing the man as one of the policemen who had guarded the hospital after the midnight shooting, I invited them in.

The girl spoke English quite well. She quickly explained their reason for coming: "I have a check from a friend in California. Would you cash it for me this morning before we leave?"

My reaction was, *Careful there, Mary!* Then the passage I had just read flashed into my mind. My

Bible still lay open to Jesus' words in Matthew 25.

"Yes, I'd be glad to," I said with only a moment's hesitation.

As the girl signed the check, I brought her Thai money at the present rate of exchange. The policeman thanked me profusely. "You have been exceptionally generous," he said with amazement. "Anywhere else she would have received only half or three-quarters of that amount."

Pointing to the Bible on my table, I showed him why I could do no less. He read the Thai text, then looked up. "Will you translate something to this girl for me?" he asked.

Turning to the young woman, the policeman laid a finger on her shoulder and said: "I want to talk to you now as a father. Daughter, twice I came to this hospital very ill. If they had not helped me, I would have died. But the doctors didn't just treat my body; they told me about God, the Father in Heaven, who loved me. Now, Daughter, you don't know what the future holds, but I commend this God to you. If you put your trust in Him, He will care for you just as He has cared for me."

It was a soul-stirring moment. My heart sang as I translated those words from Thai into English, words spoken by a man who had often asked about Jesus Christ, but who had never before openly professed his belief.

Later that morning police opened the way for us to minister to two more groups of refugees still in the district, one billeted in a public-health facility, the other at a Buddhist temple. While collecting items to take to the refugees, I picked a very large papaya from a tree in my back yard. *What a beautiful papaya!* I thought. *Maybe I should keep it for myself.* Rejecting the temptation, I laid the fruit in my basket. When we reached the temple, I found many refugees ill and dehydrated. God knew how much their bodies needed a papaya that had just that day tree-ripened to perfection.

On returning home that afternoon, I went to collect my mail and found a parcel of biscuit mix, mailed from the States three months earlier. Back at the house, the cook jubilantly held up a little bottle of honey she had bought that morning! Because honey rarely appeared in our local market, we laughed together when I showed her the box of biscuit mix.

After a delicious supper of biscuits and honey I climbed the stairs to the apartment of our Thai evangelist to share the day's happenings with her. Interrupting me, she said, "I know about your morning visitors. That policeman brought his wife to see the doctor this morning. He came looking for you. He said that he and the woman for whom you cashed the check got back to the police station just in time for her to catch the truck taking the refugees to their new location. Telling me what happened at your house, he said, 'Now I know without doubt these doctors are here to help us and not for gain of their own.'"

The evangelist continued: "He had his Bible, wrapped in newspaper, under his arm. He unwrapped it and opened it to the text you had shown him and said, 'It's true! If we do justly to others and help them, it's like doing it to Jesus!'"

When the evangelist had finished telling her story, she went to a drawer and drew out some money. Handing it to me, she said, "This is tithe; I want it to be used for the refugees." With tears she admitted she had considered dipping into it for something personal. "But now I want it to be used for others." We wept together, and I thanked God for abundantly answering my morning's "What can I do for You?" request.

A month later I had other unexpected visitors—this time a former nurse's aide and her husband, now living in California. When they mentioned that their home was in San Diego, I told them about the check I had cashed for a refugee on a bank there.

"What bank was it?" they asked.

I went for the check. One look and they exclaimed, "Why, that's our bank!" They offered to give me money for the check and then take it back with them to cash when they got home. Later they wrote saying they had no problem cashing the well-traveled check. How thrilling to see God work out the details in the things we do "as unto Him"!

Though each group of refugees stayed with us only two or three weeks, and though communication was limited, we became friends as I ministered to their needs. I always felt sad when a group moved on. Most I would never see again. But one day I shall meet some of them in that place without language barrier or time constraint. There, we will rejoice together in all Christ has done for us!

Looking back on those days, I am thankful that God not only kept to His promise, but helped me keep to mine. ■

ఴ35ఆ
An Era Closes

I had no sooner returned to Saiburi for my eighth and last term of missionary service in Asia than Dr. John Garland, the hospital superintendent, met me with a request: "Mary, many guests are coming through these days, and we need someone to coordinate their visits. Would you consider doing this for us?"

Scarcely giving me time to consider the idea, he continued: "The business manager is capably caring for the refugees now, and the recent directive from the Thai Education Department restricts the training of nurse's aides, even for our own hospital. Would you do this other job? It *just* means finding places in our missionary homes for visitors."

Knowing how the continuing shortage of missionary medical personnel was saddling everyone with heavy workloads, I could not refuse to add hostessing to my duties at the hospital.

*E*arly in that final term, changes began to squeeze our work at the hospital like a powerful wringer. New government quotas made replacing missionary medical personnel virtually impossible. Although officials later rescinded the restricting order about the training of nurse's aides, it had generated fears not easily reversed. Questions from every quarter multiplied. "What will happen now?" "Will the hospital have to close? If so, when?" "What about our jobs?"

We could give no simple answers. Clearly the future of the hospital was in jeopardy and with it the jobs of over a hundred national employees. Pedicab drivers who for years had made a satisfactory living transporting patients and others to and from the hospital would also suffer if the hospital shut down. Merchants and townspeople felt threatened as well. Uncertainly bred an undercurrent of bitterness.

*A*s concerns spread, patients, many with long-standing needs, flooded the hospital. The influx so taxed the physical and emotional resources of our nurse's aides that some began looking elsewhere for less stressful employment. Private hospitals in the area, aware of their excellent training, hired them eagerly.

As overload intensified, we knew we had to lessen the burden on the remaining staff. But how? Should we close the hospital altogether on a certain date, or should we phase the operation down gradually? Day by day we sought the mind of Christ, our Burden Bearer, and step by step He led us.

As demands on our capable Australian midwife became impossibly heavy, we tried to limit hospital deliveries to local residents only. When that failed to cut patient load sufficiently, we closed the midwifery department entirely, consoling ourselves that expectant mothers could now find facilities in nearby government hospitals and clinics.

Still later, because of continuing loss of nurse's aides, we had to reduce the number of in-patient beds. To compensate, we expanded out-patient facilities.

We reserved the remaining in-patient beds for acutely ill or dangerously injured patients. That meant we had no beds in the hospital for a fellow missionary or a child of a national staff member needing care. Already stretched medical missionary staff sacrificially opened their homes as temporary havens for ill or recuperating fellow workers. Our reduced nurse's aide staff shouldered extra duties so that fellow aides could take time off to care for a sick child or parent at home.

Those were days of deep heart searching for those of us who had served at the little hospital from its beginning. We had watched it grow into an effective center for conscientious care and gospel outreach. We desperately needed wisdom and a loving respect for those who challenged the changes. Many believed that "their hospital" would always be there for them. We, too, wished it could have been so.

*T*hough still involved in the challenges within the hospital, I faced change as well in my hostessing duties outside the hospital. Our facilities now became a venue for other mission activities. The grassy grounds, volley-ball court and the nearby beach soon rang with the shouts and laughter of youth and children's camps. Old classrooms buzzed with planning sessions, seminars, days of prayer, conferences, and weekend Bible schools for missionaries and national Christians. Men and boys bunked in empty wards in the hospital, women and girls in former student dormitories.

Holding our annual five-day conference for all south Thailand missionaries at Saiburi meant extra work for those of us living at the hospital. But doctors and nurses could more easily attend at least some of the sessions. Often duties had kept them from participating in earlier conferences held further away.

At one larger than usual conference, jammed accommodations gave everyone an experience in living "closer than the pages of a book," as someone expressed it. That week, with our faithful house-helpers working flat out, we managed to prepare and cater over 760 meals from my tiny apartment kitchen. Happily all conferees survived!

*O*ver the years, in the close give-and-take of life at Saiburi Christian Hospital, I formed strong personal relationships with individuals from every ethnic group in the region. When someone turned from spiritual darkness to light in Christ, my joy soared.

When one and another lost interest in God's gracious gift of salvation or rejected it outright, I watched with deepening pain.

Every life that touched mine made my life richer. I smile to remember the times we laughed and frolicked at games or picnics, celebrated at weddings, rejoiced in the birth of a baby, or delighted in scholastic milestones reached. Those happy events outshine the discordant, heartbreaking times. But all combined to create the tapestry God had planned for my life.

Change, sometimes unwelcome, shaped the path of God's leading in my thirty-eight years of service in China and Thailand. Now the time had come for a very different change—retirement. It was not easy to leave the Asia that had become my home and say goodbye to the people closest to me.

My final days at Saiburi brimmed with activities—sad-sweet visits, dinners, parties, speeches, and prayers—and tears. One memory stands out: At the last weekly missionary prayer meeting I attended our senior surgeon, Dr. Rupert Clark, well-known for his brief and to-the-point prayers, had been asked to pray. After voicing the usual requests for someone retiring, he concluded with, "And, Lord, keep Mary from becoming a sour, crotchety old woman!" Snorts of stifled laughter from the assembled company drowned out *his* "amen," but not *mine*—a hearty, sincere one! That's a prayer I continue to lay before the Lord.

As the van drove me through the hospital gates one last time, bearing me away from my palm-shaded Saiburi home of twenty-five years, my heart burst with

gratitude for every manifestation of God's inex-
haustable mercy and grace. It was He who had
worked in me "to will and to do of his good pleasure"
(Ph. 2:13). It was He who enabled me to keep the
promise I made to Him as a child those many years
ago. ∎

Look on the Fields

Many more challenges and victories await the young missionaries of the 21st century as they follow in the footsteps of pioneers like Mary Teegardin. Since Mary's years in China the China Inland Mission, now known as OMF International, has spread across eighteen countries in East Asia—home to almost two billion people. Fewer than five percent know Christ. Today nearly one thousand dedicated OMF missionaries are giving their energies to spread the Good News among this massive enclave of the unreached. Asia's needs today demand the innovation and commitment of modern Mary Teegardins, armed as she was with God's Spirit.

The men and women of OMF are pioneers skilled to function in modern society and ready to make the most of their opportunities to share Christ. But pioneering isn't the whole story. Our goal is a biblical church for every Asian community worldwide. Where no churches exist, we seek to plant them. Where the church is established, we assist its ministry and encourage its development.

When Mary Teegardin went to China and Thailand, she depended on the power of God. Nothing has changed. The same power still opens closed minds, softens unbelieving hearts, and radically changes lives.

Satellite communications and the internet provide an immediate link to Asia, but they are no match for the power of prayer brought to life through men and women like you. Through your prayers God changes otherwise immovable circumstances, strengthens weary saints, and draws people into a personal relationship with Himself.

Will you pray with us for the lost of Asia and for those who seek to reach them? Will you be one of the 21st century Mary Teegardins whom God will use to draw unreached people to Himself?

Want to know more? To learn how you can be a part of this great challenge, contact your nearest OMF office at the address below:

U.S.A. 10 W. Dry Creek Circle
Littleton, CO 80120
800-422-5330

Canada 5759 Coopers Avenue
Mississauga, ON L4Z 1R9
905-568-9971

Britain Station Approach, Borough Green
Sevenoaks, Kent TN15 8BG

Australia PO Box 849, Epping, NSW 2121
61(2)9868-4777

Asia 2 Cluny Road, Singapore 259570
Republic of Singapore
65(475)4592

More books from CLC

World Prayer
Will Bruce, J. Hudson Taylor, J.O. Fraser, J.O. Sanders
Where are the boundaries of your world—your
Jerusalem, your Judea, your Samaria? Let the
visionary prayer of J. Hudson Taylor, the practical
prayer tools of Will Bruce, the life of abiding prayer of
J. Oswald Sanders, and the prayer of faith of J.O.
Fraser enlarge the boundaries of your prayer life to
encompass the full scope of God's heart for the world.

Stronger than the Strong
Louise Morris
OMF has volumes of stories of God working in
wondrous ways to establish His church among
unreached peoples. One of the most moving is the
story of Jim and Louise Morris. They knew the pain of
years of labor without fruit. When would God fulfill
His promise?

Every Good Gift
Linda Baker-Kaahanui
In 1949 Mao Zedong stood in Tiananmen Square and
announced that China was now a communist country.
What happened during the next 30 years of silence? In
spite of systematic elimination and persecution, each
Christian has multiplied into 100 Christians. This book
is titled *Every Good Gift* for a reason. James 1:17 tells
us, "Every good gift and every perfect gift is from
above ... ." Come meet some people who have none of
the accouterments of Christianity ... but have found
everything they need in God alone.

More books from OMF

Behind the Ranges
Geraldine Taylor
J.O. Fraser's heroic spirit comes to life in this classic
biography, which includes excerpts from his letters
and journals. This is a picture of one of Christ's
outstanding and unusual disciples—outstanding in
his determination to serve only one master and
unusual in his abandon to the life and conditions of
those to whom he went, the Lisu of people of China.

Ascent to the Tribes
Isobel Kuhn
Day was breaking on the Thailand hills. A sense of
something new coming had been scattered over the
mountaintops. A new name, the name of Jesus, was
heard on the lips of tribe after tribe.

Second-Mile People
Isobel Kuhn
This is the last of Isobel Kuhn's many books. The
manuscript was discovered tucked away in a big file
several years after her death by cancer. These six
"second-mile people" were friends and colleagues
whose lives made a deep impression on Isobel. These
lives were, as she put it, "Splendid meteors trailing
such radiance after them that something of their own
celestial fire has sought to enter into us also."

BROOKHAVEN
WESLEYAN CHURCH
2960 E. 38th & Garthwaite
Marion, Indiana 46952

266.1   #340
Tee   Teegardin, Mary.
          A promise is to keep

DATE DUE

9/6/03			
5/28			

BROOKHAVEN
WESLEYAN CHURCH
2960 E. 38th & Garthwaite
Marion, Indiana 46952

DEMCO